Shared
Manufacturing

Shared Manufacturing

A Global Perspective

Bopaya Bidanda
School of Engineering
University of Pittsburgh
Pittsburgh, Pennsylvania

David I. Cleland
School of Engineering
University of Pittsburgh
Pittsburgh, Pennsylvania

Shriram R. Dharwadkar
School of Engineering Technology
South Carolina State University
Orangeburg, South Carolina

McGraw-Hill, Inc.
New York   San Francisco   Washington, D.C.   Auckland   Bogotá
Caracas   Lisbon   London   Madrid   Mexico City   Milan
Montreal   New Delhi   San Juan   Singapore
Sydney   Tokyo   Toronto

Library of Congress Cataloging-in-Publication Data

Bidanda, Bopaya.
   Shared manufacturing : a global perspective / Bopaya Bidanda,
David I. Cleland, Shriram R. Dharwadkar.
      p.   cm.
   Includes index.
   ISBN 0-07-157812-9
   1. Manufactures—Technological innovations. 2. Production
engineering—Technological innovations. 3. Technology transfer.
4. Production management. I. Cleland, David I. II. Dharwadkar,
Shriram R. III. Title.
TS149.B52   1993
658.5—dc20   93-17324
                                    CIP

1 2 3 4 5 6 7 8 9 0 DOC/DOC 9 9 8 7 6 5 4 3

ISBN 0-07-157812-9

*The sponsoring editor for this book is Larry S. Hager, the editing
supervisor is Joseph Bertuna, and the production supervisor is
Pamela A. Pelton. It was set in Century Schoolbook by
McGraw-Hill's Professional Book Group composition unit.*

Printed and bound by R. R. Donnelley & Sons Company.

This book is printed on recycled, acid-free paper containing a minimum of 50% recycled de-
inked fiber.

Contents

Foreword

The Cold War was about freedom, and America won. The "trade war" is about jobs and living standards, and America is faltering. In recent years, millions of good-paying manufacturing jobs have moved abroad—500,000 jobs lost in textiles and apparel, another 600,000 in steel and automobiles. The once mighty U.S. consumer electronics industry has disappeared virtually in its entirety. Imports have seized 57 percent of the U.S. market for machine tools. These losses, in turn, have propelled a shocking decline in the U.S. standard of living, with wages falling 20 percent over the last 20 years.

U.S. manufacturers face unprecedented challenges in meeting the competition from abroad. They must improve quality, boost productivity, reduce costs, and speed the commercialization of products and services. Already, U.S. manufacturing has undergone profound changes—changes in hardware, software, information technology, alternative organization designs, and the role of both managers and production workers.

Mass production, the great locomotive of U.S. manufacturing throughout the 20th century, is giving way to *lean manufacturing*. Flexible manufacturing systems have transformed the whole structure of the manufacturing enterprise. Concurrent engineering and advanced computer networks are linking up factory jobs, design engineering, suppliers, and customers in dynamic new arrangements. .

Small and midsized manufacturers, which account for the majority of American producers, lag far behind global competitors in utilizing modern manufacturing systems technology. Federal and state aid to these manufacturers has been modest compared to the billions of dollars in financial support extended to foreign rivals by governments in Europe and the Pacific Rim. Although expanded support to U.S. manufacturers may be forthcoming from both federal and state initiatives, self-help will be a key factor in improving American competitiveness.

Shared manufacturing is a viable strategy for assisting small and midsized manufacturers in sharpening their competitive edge. In this timely book, Professors Bidanda, Cleland, and Dharwadkar provide an overview of the experiences of both the United States and foreign countries in using shared manufacturing centers to develop and transfer systems technology. This book also offers a paradigm for building a network of shared manufacturing centers within a given manufacturing community. This paradigm offers promise not just to specific manufacturing communities but also to the larger task of enhancing America's national productivity and competitiveness.

Ernest F. Hollings
United States Senator

Preface

The awesome challenges facing U.S. manufacturers have been chronicled in professional, trade, and popular press publications. In this book we continue to describe some of the strategic issues and challenges that face manufacturers today, in particular the small and midsized manufacturers who have limited equipment, computer resources, skilled people, and finances to keep up with the state of the art in their manufacturing operations. As a result of these shortcomings, these manufacturers are in critical need of assistance to be able to compete and survive in the unforgiving global manufacturing markets. Although the main focus of this book is on U.S. manufacturing, the concept of shared manufacturing has application to any industrial society. As emerging nations seek to gain a presence in manufacturing, the use of shared manufacturing to assist small and midsized manufacturers to improve their global competitiveness is a rational and needed strategy.

All too many small and midsized manufacturers are being consistently beaten in domestic and international markets in the areas of manufacturing process development and implementation. Survival of these manufacturers requires access to state-of-the-art equipment and professional consultancy services. The limited finances of such manufacturers preclude their being able to make any substantial progress in improving quality and productivity, reducing cost, and commercializing products on a competitive basis without some form of assistance.

New techniques in manufacturing have outdated many time-proven traditional manufacturing strategies—many of which were based on assembly line and job shop techniques. Product-process design teams, production teams, computer integrated manufacturing, materials requirements planning, just-in-time inventory, and flexible manufacturing systems are a few of the major changes stalking U.S. manufacturers. Small and midsized manufacturers need a local center where they can go to obtain professional assistance in modern manufacturing systems technology through the use of a manufacturing facility shared with other manufacturers who face similar problems and challenges.

This book provides an overview of the concept and experiences found in the use of shared manufacturing centers. At the start the reader is reminded of some of the more striking global manufacturing realities—and how one manufacturing community assessed its needs for justifying and establishing a shared manufacturing assistance center (SMAC)—a center devoted to the transfer of manufacturing systems technology. Then the book recommends some strategies for the configuration and equipping of a SMAC—and how the use of project management concepts and processes can be used to manage the development and start-up of a SMAC. Following this, an overall management systems model for shared manufacturing initiatives is given. Three overseas shared manufacturing initiatives are then described—Germany, Taiwan, and France. A modest shared manufacturing center operating in western Pennsylvania in the tool and die industry is discussed. Finally, the concluding chapter revisits some of the major issues and challenges facing U.S. small and midsize manufacturers—and how a blend of federal, state, and local assistance can be marshaled to serve the needs of manufacturing communities desiring to improve the efficiency and effectiveness of their manufacturing businesses.

The book ends on two important thoughts: First, that a *network of shared manufacturing centers in the United States will provide a place where manufacturers can regain and improve their global competitiveness.* Second, a shared manufacturing center is offered as a means of coping with the likely provision of government assistance from the Clinton Administration to help needy manufacturers—and how a self-help program of building alliances with local manufacturers and educational institutions can be successful even if unlikely—and improbable—substantial funding comes from federal, state, and local governments.

Acknowledgments

The authors have elected to have several chapters written by leading experts in the field of concepts, strategies, and techniques of shared manufacturing. These experts have shown how shared manufacturing strategies are carried out in some countries that have been notably successful in using shared manufacturing centers to enhance national and global competitiveness. One chapter describes how a shared manufacturing center in western Pennsylvania was developed. Finally, a chapter offers key strategies on how to manage a shared manufacturing center. The experts that have helped in developing this book include:

Ted Lettes and Tip Parker, U.S. Department of Commerce, Washington, D.C., "Economics, Management Policies, and Accounting Practices for a Shared Flexible Computer Integrated Manufacturing Facility."

H.C. Mult, Günter Spur, and Rita Pokorny, Production Technology Center Berlin, Germany, "The Berlin Institute for Production Systems and Design Technology as a Model for the Concept of the Fraunhofer Society in Germany."

Ching Wen Li, National Taipei Institute of Technology, "Small and Medium Sized Industries in R.O.C.: A Model Policy for Continued Growth."

Pierre Padilla, Centre Technique des Industries Mecaniques, Senlis, France, "CETIM: A Shared Manufacturing Model in France."

David M. Porreca, National Institute of Flexible Manufacturing, Meadville, Pa., "Shared Manufacturing: The American Experience."

We thank these experts for their willingness to contribute to this book on shared manufacturing—a "first of its kind" strategic initiative. All have had substantial experience in the workings of shared manufacturing facilities. Their contributions reflect a wide range of professionalism and viewpoints in the growing and important body of knowledge of shared manufacturing.

We thank the members of the University of Pittsburgh Manufacturing Assistance Center (MAC) team who have worked so arduously in the conceptualization and development of that center. Over several years these team members include Mitch Berg, Ken Kahn, Carie Mullins, Mehmet Gulsen, Chris Chung, Chalice Zavada, Rick Billo, and Matt Berardi. In discussions with these people surfaced many ideas and initiatives to meld into the evolving strategy for our MAC. We also thank our many friends in the Greater Pittsburgh manufacturing community who provided a willing and competent forum for the discussions of strategies for the development and implementation of the MAC in western Pennsylvania.

We are deeply indebted to Clair Zubritzky, who provided her usual superlative assistance in the administrative matters involved in this book. We would also like to thank Mr. Cenk Tunasar and Mr. Jim Peternel for providing some of the original artwork for Chap. 3, 4, and 8. Special thanks to Dr. Harvey W. Wolfe, chairman of the Industrial Engineering Department, and Dr. Charles A. Sorber, Dean of the School of Engineering of the University of

Pittsburgh, who provided us with the resources and environment to pursue this book. And, we thank those people who will read this book—and in so doing be better prepared to encourage the development of shared manufacturing strategies in their environments.

Bopaya Bidanda
David I. Cleland
Shriram R. Dharwadkar

Shared
Manufacturing

1

Global
Manufacturing
Realities

In the past several years, the changes that have come about in the global economic community have been awesome. Quality and speed have become the entry fee in the global markets. Business organizations are undergoing change, the implications of which are just being felt. Manufacturing has long been a productive contributor to the economic well-being of the United States. Manufacturing competition in the global markets has posed strategic challenges to the United States, or any other nation, to survive in world markets without a renaissance in manufacturing strategy. Indeed, manufacturing stands on the threshold of a new world order in which national boundaries become less important than the ability of the manufacturing organization to find and secure its competitive place in the world. The ability to plan for change will be characteristic of those companies that prosper; those companies that do not plan for continuous improvement in the conceptualization and implementation of innovative state-of-the-art manufacturing systems will be marginal competitors. Failure is a more likely destiny for companies that fail to plan.

The competitive dimension in the ability to deliver quality products through effective organizational processes to global customers is the name of the game today. Much has been developed in innovative manufacturing systems technology: CAD, CAE, CAM, JIT, TQM, MAP, MRP, and such innovations that promise solutions to the improvement of manufacturing go on and on. Simultaneous engineering, employee participation, production teams, and such new ways of aligning and using manufacturing resources continue to come forth from around the world.

In this chapter we capture some of the major dimensions of global manufacturing. In so doing we bring forth the idea that all too many U.S. manufacturers are being left behind because of the lack of wherewithal to compete in the world markets. Small and midsized manufacturers contribute greatly in the ability of original equipment manufacturers (OEMs) to develop, manufacture, and market world-class products and services. In the United States we believe these manufacturers need help in order for them to more fully realize their potential. Accordingly, this book suggests some strategies that can help such manufacturers: through the process of *shared manufacturing*.

Before the concept and process of shared manufacturing is presented, a summary review of the conditions and the reality of global manufacturing is needed.

Global Changes

In the new competitive global marketplace a shift is occurring from wealth determined from natural resources to wealth from technology and knowledge. A form of "intellectual wealth" has emerged where the effective and efficient management of people has become the principal focus of competitiveness. Yet the creation of wealth through a technology can vanish overnight, as happened when the FAX put the kibosh on the telex technology. Established wealth in computer technology can be lost quickly if the company is not able to beat the technology offered by the competitors. Competition in that industry is extraordinary. One computer company described a key corporate objective as "leapfrog the technology every three years." The attainment of such an objective can put competitors under unusual pressure to match, and exceed, the technology offered in the marketplace.

Another characteristic of the global basis for competing is the growing attitude that there are no products per se—rather a customer should be provided with a "bundle of services" to include the product, its after-sales service, and ongoing consultation in the use of the product *and* the expectation that products embodying advanced technology will be forthcoming. This requires a change of attitude on the part of managers and professionals. Manufacturers that thrive into the next generation will compete by providing a bundle of services with products that respond to customer needs. Downstream activities such as after-sales service will be joined by how well manufacturers are able to serve customers during the product-design process. Businesses will be competing more and more on services in the future.[1]

The idea of a "bundle of services" can take competition a step beyond total quality and total customer service. It also keynotes the idea of "ownership" of the customer in that the company does not want its relationship with the customer to end when the product has been purchased. For example, Lexus works to maintain its relationship with its customers throughout the time that the automobile is owned. The Ford Motor Company has a policy of assessing the quality of customer service during the time the customer owns the car. Federal Express maintains a 24-hour consumer line for tracing packages for customers as a step toward total customer service.

The idea of providing a bundle of services to the customer is catching on with vendors. In the long run, companies are slowly recognizing that it does pay to take advantage of suppliers. The new philosophy is a "win-win" relationship in the form of a "strategic alliance" where the suppliers get the advantage of a long-term contract and the customer gets the security of a committed supplier willing to cast fortune with the customer. Somewhat like a "blanket purchase order," the customer is able to call on the supplier for parts and services without the drudgery of renegotiating the contract. Bringing in suppliers to serve on the customer's product-design team to work together in the design of products and processes has had special benefits such as the reduction of incoming inspections, a window on new technologies, and a commitment to work together in the competitive marketplace. When the purchasing professions work together closely with a few select, prequalified suppliers, there are opportunities to reduce costs, save time, improve quality, and benefit from the technological understanding of the vendors.

When the company thinks about providing customers with a bundle of services rather than just a product, opportunities for economies in the whole producer-customer relationship and transaction are possible. This happened when Xerox redefined its business as document processing and GE developed its slogan of "GE and its customers—one system, not two systems."

Global markets and competitive realities are blurring the concept of the nation-state. The power of information and technology, closer relationships between suppliers and customers, new workplace realities and work force demographics are changing the implicit contract about the relationships between employers and employees. Companies will find it necessary to work on projects in which countries and profit center divisions combine forces. Leadership will also involve thinking across boundaries.[2]

Global competitors have invested in advanced manufacturing technologies, developed new R&D initiatives, and launched innovations in manufacturing management and production control practices. In doing this, these competitors have benefited from more supportive public policies than have been available in the United States. In addition, these overseas competitors have had greater access to capital and lower interest rates, stronger tax incentives for modernization, a significantly higher proportion of private funding devoted to R&D funding directed to manufacturing technologies, and widely available loan guarantees for smaller manufacturers. As a result some of our leading competitor nations have been able to modernize their manufacturing infrastructure more rapidly than the United States, thereby gaining a significant lead in manufacturing competitiveness in areas such as:

- Quality of manufactured products
- Optimization of manufacturing technologies
- Shorter product-development cycles
- Introduction of automation technologies
- Technical sophistication of the work force[3]

National boundaries in manufacturing have become less important than the strategies needed to master the marketplace.

Across the Borders

Today, corporate strategic decisions about manufacturing and business locations are driven by the realities of global competition, not by national alliances. Cross-border ownership is accelerating, with manufacturing location decisions being made on where the greatest advantage can be gained.[4]

Kenichi Ohmae's *The Borderless World* makes an important case of the growing dominance of consumers over companies and countries, and of the eroding and merging of national economic borders. On a competitive map that shows the real flows of financial and industrial activity, he shows that national boundaries have largely disappeared. Performance standards for products and processes are now set in the global marketplace by those who buy the products, not those who make them. This means that managers have to reconsider how their companies develop new products and processes. It also means that companies that survive and grow must be truly global and decentralized and must focus on what the market needs.[5]

In a comprehensive survey of 12,000 managers from around the world, Kanter found that instantaneous communication, the globalization of markets, travel at the speed of sound, political realignments, changing demographics, technological changes in both products and processes, global strategic alliances, and the flattening of organizations—all of the foregoing and more are changing the structure and strategies of organizations. "The once very rigid and unbreachable boundaries of business are fading in the face of change."[6]

In managing borderless manufacturing systems the building of strategic alliances to share markets and resources is required. Changes in the global economy have heightened and contributed to the trend of strategic alliances to include the following:

- Improved communication and transportation systems which have extended the global reach of domestic companies
- Increased competition among multinationals which requires innovative approaches to deal with new market entrants and increased competitive pressures
- Dramatic foreign exchange revaluations affecting comparative production and inventory costs and international investment flows
- The need for technology sharing and other resource sharing as a precondition for participating in global markets

The development of products and supporting processes will be one of the key competitive factors in the 1990s. This means that the ability to commercialize technology will be as important as the traditional economies of scale, skilled labor, possession of proprietary technology, and access to capital and markets. Some companies will compete by entering into strategic alliances in the development of products. In others the alliance will be built on the sharing of marketing and manufacturing resources.

The United States faces particular challenges in competing in global manufacturing.

U.S. Manufacturing

Manufacturing in the United States is of great importance. It accounts for about 23 percent of GNP and about 75 percent of all U.S. exports; it provides about 19 million jobs. U.S. manufacturing is facing a new future caused by the convergence of several important trends that include:

- The spread of manufacturing capabilities worldwide
- The emergence of advanced manufacturing systems technologies
- Growing changes in management systems, labor practices, and manufacturing cultures

National remedial changes are under way in the United States, some of which are being undertaken at the national level.

On March 20, 1991, the Council on Competitiveness, an industry-academic-labor group, published a report supportive of a partnership of government and business to boost America's eroding industrial strength. The report advances the hypothesis that economic growth is driven by a set of critical technologies, advanced structural materials, biotechnology, microelectronics, computers, and software. The report puts much of the onus for improving competitiveness on matching or surpassing the best global product commercialization practices. The report further notes that effort must be more focused on the sorts of generic precompetitive R&D that small and medium-sized companies can convert into saleable products.

The U.S. government and industry combined still spend more on R&D than any other nation. Many projects appear to lack practicality, such as the bulk of the $7 billion in Energy Department research that is done in the department's labs, which are largely isolated from U.S. industry. What is needed is an approach more like that taken in Japan, where government-sponsored research done to maximize market impact is the norm. The Japanese companies share in the discoveries and go on to compete aggressively in product-process development.[7]

A large part of the U.S. dilemma in manufacturing stems from continued acceptance of traditional manufacturing practices. The Clinton Administration has taken concrete steps to develop a proactive national technology policy in manufacturing and has initiated steps to incorporate government involvement in manufacturing.

Traditional Manufacturing

The battles of manufacturing are being fought on a global battlefield. This war demands products of a world-class quality; it demands the ability to create innovative products and processes. It requires, as never before, the ability to reduce costs, to manage inventory, and to create a new class of manufacturing worker. It puts a premium on the ability to respond quickly to changing customers' needs using new technologies. Old-fashioned traditional manufacturing organizations and facilities are inefficient and costly to maintain and can be a handicap to the development of new products and manufacturing processes.

The principles of traditional manufacturing, based on decades of manufacturing using traditional methods, have prevailed for too long. Traditional manufacturing principles that have served the manufacturing community well for decades include:

- *Marketing dominance* in the setting of demand for the production of products to sell at a certain price.

- *Over the wall* product-process design strategies where design engineering designed the products and handed the product over to manufacturing to build and then on to marketing to sell.

- *First-level supervisors* or bosses who tell workers what to do. Rigid job classifications restrict workers to performing one or a few tasks on the production line, resulting in a dehumanizing culture with rigid rules where the workers have no stake or pride in the manufacturing processes.

- *Large inventories* with buffer stocks maintained at each stage of the manufacturing process to ensure that the assembly line is kept moving.

- *Quality is "inspected in"* the product as inspectors on the production line check specifications, reject bad parts, or send the parts off to another section of the manufacturing facility for repair.

- *Distributors,* part of the wholesaler-retailer network, exist to serve the customers, and receive large amounts of products which are warehoused to provide buffers for fluctuation in customer demands.

- *Unionized work force,* which through their elected union representatives negotiated the terms and conditions of the workplace. Participation by the workers in influencing their conditions of work was limited. There was little feeling of product-process ownership by the employees. (Paraphrased from Ref. 8.)

Change in the way that manufacturing is managed is under way. The wave of downsizing and restructuring by U.S. manufacturing firms in the 1980s reflects the past sins of building too many layers of managers in American businesses. It also reflects the growing awareness by manufacturers of new models of economies of scale, requiring new marketing approaches, new product-process development strategies, and innovative management styles. It also reflects adaptive organizational designs and the ability of all companies to "think small" in the sense of creating within existing organizational structures the small organizational unit where a better chance exists for creativity and innovation to flourish, unhampered by the bureaucratic organization. Competitive advantage will be gained through the ability to automate manufacturing and the ability to find ways to more effectively use the knowledge and skills of *all* people in the organization, from the CEO to the workers on the production line.

Business is retreating from the bureaucratic "command and control" mind-set of the past to a "consensus and consent" system of values appropriate for today's fast-changing environment. In this environment, knowledge and employee empowerment provide the leavening for organizational success.

American manufacturers are pursuing additional remedial strategies. The global manufacturing community is entering a decade of unprecedented competitive pressures and the emergence of bold new manufacturing management and technological initiatives. U.S. manufacturers are accused by many of having already lost their place as the world's technological leader. To revitalize their competitiveness, American manufacturers are pursuing remedial strategies such as:

- Modification of existing organizational structures to a more flexible, adaptive organization where the strategies to respond to change are brought to a focus through cross-functional project teams, particularly in the concurrent design of products and supporting processes.

- Senior management is developing a familiarity with the new manufacturing management and technological possibilities, and then developing the *vision* for the organization to marshal its resources so that relevant information is available to the project teams that are developing and implementing new technologies and management schemas.

- Senior management is taking an active part in evaluating the adequacy of the work being undertaken by cross-functional teams through providing supporting resources, inspiration, and ongoing surveillance over the adequacy of the work being carried out by the teams.

- Improvement of manufacturing operational strategies is being done through maximum use of flexible manufacturing systems, just-in-time (JIT) inventory management, and the other recent innovations in manufacturing that are becoming the hallmarks of global manufacturing.

- Recognizing that the best technology does not always do the job, people who have to interface with the machines and the software are being trained to improve their knowledge, skills, and attitudes. This means an aggressive and comprehensive educational program that prepares all people for the change, from senior executives to the shop-floor workers.

One survey noted that some U.S. manufacturers are truly becoming formidable competitors, but some of the potential major players lack the commitment and aggressiveness to globalize their businesses and start shaping world markets.[9] Coleman[10] noted that:

- U.S. manufacturers have finally recognized that their competitors are across the ocean, not across the street.

- Too many manufacturers still hesitate to implement the kind of far-reaching changes that will be required to achieve global superiority.

- Enlightened American manufacturers have made great progress in developing and integrating a global strategy, establishing manufacturing facilities worldwide to capitalize on monetary fluctuations, centralizing strategic decisions on manufacturing and logistics, establishing new facilities in growth markets, and using advanced philosophies such as JIT and total quality commitment.

Although many executives have taken the first steps toward a world-class manufacturing capability, a significant number don't expect to complete the process until the late 1990s. That may be too late.

The United States is making real progress in improving its competitive stand in manufacturing. The last three or four years have helped. The decline of the American dollar since late 1985 has made U.S. goods more competitive. Business costs have been reduced through company downsizing, restructuring, and refocusing. Progress has been made in the following ways, but there is still a long way to go.

- Labor costs have been reduced through the use of automated production facilities.

- Outsourcing has increased, becoming global for a wide range of parts, components, and subsystems.

- Plant sizes have been reduced, plants have been closed, and manufacturing capacity has shrunk, leading to more productive manufacturing operations.

- Wage increases have slowed significantly; employees have become more concerned about job security and, through the efforts of enlightened management, are being empowered to become true partners along with managers and professionals in influencing the destiny of the firm.

Global strategies in manufacturing are slowly being adopted in the United States. The thinking is changing. Some manufacturers are putting the factories where they are needed.

Global Strategies

When doing business with global partners it is necessary to think and act like your competitors. James Morgan, CEO of Applied Materials, Inc., is just such a realist. He concluded in the late 1970s that the semiconductor business was shifting to Japan. By 1980, he had established Applied Materials Japan, staffed almost entirely by Japanese personnel. By keeping his products up to date with painstaking care he learned how to do business with the Japanese. By virtue of being located in Japan, Morgan's engineers and scientists are able to spend time with Japanese semiconductor makers to find out how to use Applied's machines. Morgan and his technical staff often customize products for specific customers in Japan. Applied Materials' competitors continued to do things the traditional way—using Japanese partners to market their wares. Over time these competitors found that their partners replaced their products with those of Japanese equipment makers as soon as comparable Japanese products became available. Applied Materials alone retained its Japanese customers.[11]

By building factories in the American heartland, the Japanese are steadily threatening the American car industry. They have also set up factories, engineering centers, design studios, and research facilities—in short everything needed to create, manufacture, and sell cars. It is a strategic move on their part—truly one of history's great transfers of industrial wealth and power. In product development and technology the Japanese have stepped out ahead of Detroit; catching up by Detroit may not be possible. Some soothsayers are predicting that the Japanese auto industry will overtake the United States in the 1990s and assume undisputed leadership by the end of the century.[12] In addition to moving its industrial base, Japan is now not hesitant in criticizing the United States.

"Americans, especially American corporations, seem to have lost their knack for invention and have forgotten how to produce things." Sony CEO Akio Morita and his coauthor, Japanese journalist Shintaro Ishihara, have had some rough things to say about the demise of the United States as a world-class manufacturing power. Some of the reasons they give include: "Americans today make money by handling money and shuffling it around, instead of creating and producing goods with some actual value....When people forget how to produce goods, and that appears to be the case in America, they will not be able to supply themselves with their most basic needs....*The time will never again come when America will regain its strength in industry.*" (Ref. 13, emphasis added.)

Some representative company strategies are showing the way for improved competitiveness in manufacturing.

Company Strategies

- Mazda's new sports car, the Miata, was designed in California and financed from Tokyo and New York; its prototype was created in

England; and it was assembled in Michigan and Mexico, using advanced electronic components developed in the United States and fabricated in Japan.

- Boeing's 777 airliner is being designed in the state of Washington and Japan. It will be assembled in Seattle, Washington, with the tail cone assembly coming from Canada, special tail sections from Italy and China, and engines from England.

- The Ford Motor Company has a state-of-the-art engine factory in Mexico where more than 1000 engines per day are assembled with a quality equal to the best in the world.

- In Europe two small steel makers (one in Luxembourg and one in Belgium) improved their steel making efficiencies by producing steel products for the other. Each agreed to manufacture products that the other had produced inefficiently. As part of the alliance, each steel maker closed some uneconomic mills. Cost savings were realized in the alliance, and the products coming out of the joint effort have higher and more uniform quality.[14]

- Asea Brown Boveri (ABB), a large global company headquartered in Zurich, is awesome in its business diversity. Along one dimension the company has a distributed global network with executives operating in a decentralized mode making decisions on product strategy and performance without regard for national boundaries. Along a second dimension it is an assembly of traditionally organized national companies, serving its home market. ABB's global "matrix" holds the two dimensions together, with people working together on teams of mixed-nationality people in the business area.[15]

- Corning, Inc., provides a model of how companies that survive in the global marketplace will develop their strategy. Corning has become a global network of interrelated businesses, some consolidated, some partly owned, that share technology, facilities, and people. Joint ventures and other alliances with external partners accounted for 37 percent of net income last year. These alliances allow Corning to develop and sell new products faster. Managers in the company are relentless in their pursuit of quality—now defined as complete customer satisfaction. To help make quality a reality, the company has established partnerships that give Corning's unionized employees more influence over how the factories are run. The CEO has emphasized the sharing of technology across business units as well as technology—sharing well beyond the corporate boundaries through a worldwide network of joint ventures and alliances.

All employees of Corning are put through a 2-day quality seminar. Employees are required to spend 5 percent of their time in job-related training. Quality goals are established such as the reduction of errors by 90 percent, and all new goods and services must meet customer requirements and match or exceed the quality of any competitors' products and services.

Unionized laborers have been given more responsibility and a share of profits. Teams of workers are allowed to redesign their workplaces and decide who should work which jobs. In one plant located at Corning's Specialty Cellular Ceramics plant in Erwin, New York, a design team selected a large, open-space configuration with a high sound-dampening ceiling and plenty of windows. The production line was built so that an entire team could work within earshot of one another, rather than scattered along a traditionally configured production line 100 yards long. A total of 47 job classifications were folded into one; employees rotated through jobs weekly and earned higher pay for each new skill they learned. Quality has improved from 10,000 defective parts per million to 3 parts—and no customer has returned any products since July 1990.

In summary, the major strategies of Corning include:

- A global network of interrelated business tied together through a corporate structure, joint ventures, and strategic alliances that share resources, technology, and people.

- A relentless pursuit of quality defined as complete customer satisfaction.

- Partnerships with unionized employees that give the people more control over how the factories are run.

- Promotion of minority and ethnic diversity in the company through aggressive hiring of blacks, women, and other minorities.

- Local community investment projects to improve the local culture where the plants are located. Corning is more directly involved in its local communities than most big U.S. corporations.

- Tearing down the organizational walls between business units and making them share technology.

- Allowing teams of hourly workers to redesign their workplaces.

- Empowering employees through the formation of teams that deal with the conditions of the workplace, the planning and control of the work, and even the elimination of overtime, imposing a 2-week shutdown, redeploying workers, and cutting travel requirements.

- Establishing the policy that a quarter of each year's revenue will come from new products.[16]

Macropolitical and economic changes in the world will add momentum to global manufacturing, as in freer trade. The elimination of trade barriers through international free-trade agreements will result in economic changes in the global markets. In Europe and in the Western Hemisphere, these changes are already under way. The United States–Canada free-trade agreement of 1988, which removes trade barriers between the two nations, has already influenced the exodus of jobs, investments, and shoppers to the United States. On one level one sees a flood of weekend Canadian shoppers who cross the border to find bargains. At another level, which is difficult to quantify but believed to be potentially significant, is the movement of factories, jobs, and even company headquarters from Canada to the United States. Should the United States–Mexico free-trade agreement be implemented, similar movement of markets, consumers, and businesses can be anticipated. Free trade will be one of the results. Other results include the continuance of the building of strategic alliances between companies in the United States, Canada, and Mexico. The transfer of manufacturing facilities and manufacturing systems technology will continue.[17]

Indeed, new manufacturing philosophies are becoming the new order.

New Philosophies

During the 1980s many industrial firms charted their competitive course with changed philosophies and strategies. Typical of many companies was the need to change along three basic areas: First, a recognition of the reality of growing global competitiveness as a condition of survival. A truly domestic market by itself ceased to exist. The reality of corporate life demanded a global focus with a vision for the organization to develop its strategies within a competitive international marketplace. Managers had to develop external and internal perspectives, with the external perspective becoming increasingly important in survival and growth. Second, a means of developing a flexible, balanced organization where authority and responsibility are shared between managers who occupy positions in the hierarchy and team members who deal with forthcoming changes in the organization. In these flexible and balanced organizations operating in a boundaryless environment, dramatically increased employee empowerment is being carried out. This empowerment starts with an organizational commitment to training and education in both product and process knowledge, skills, and attitudes; included is the development of new skills needed in the flexible, balanced organization in such matters as team building, problem solving, and how to participate in the technical and managerial considerations in product-process development projects. Everyone is provided the opportunity to participate proactively at their levels in process development. Managers, long used to making all the decisions, need to develop the courage and the attitudes to seek the participation of the organization's members and be willing to go along with the judgment of people at all levels in the enterprise. The third characteristic is the elimination of real and imagined boundaries in the company and its environment. This involves breaking with the tradition of an organization with walls between its functions, and viewing all the work of the enterprise from the relative and appropriate perspective of products and supporting processes. For managers, one of their major challenges will be to select appropriate products to be developed—and in that process identify the major work processes that have to be performed by the organization to bring the products to satisfied customers. This means building project-process teams that involve all the people who contribute to the product and its supporting processes, regardless of the organizational unit that the people call "home." This will require new ways of planning, organizing, monitoring, and controlling work. The objective will be to produce a product-realization process by eliminating internal and external boundaries through the use of new ways of organizing and empowering people in using project management techniques.

These organizations will be driven by the need to accomplish organizational mission, objectives, and goals through the use of a participatively arrived at strategy. Within the organization itself speed, simplicity, and self-confidence will provide a basic organizational philosophy around which products and processes can be developed and produced.[18] Speed is the ability to develop product-process capabilities throughout a world sans boundaries. Speed also refers to the ability to act and react quickly through many boundaries in accomplishing results through the continuous empowerment of people. Simplicity is achieved by focusing on improvement of work practices—as in the execution of the simultaneous engineering function—and on the elimination of bureaucratic and technological boundaries. Self-confidence addresses people empowerment, giving them authority and expecting and demanding the assumption of responsibility in return, and providing them with the continuous opportunity to upgrade their knowledge, skills, and attitudes in their work, their organization, and themselves as members of a flexible, balanced team dealing with changes in the organization. Speed, simplicity, and self-confidence are the touchstones of the boundaryless company. Out of all this we realize the world of manufacturing is changing. Some believe these changes are something of a revolution.

The New Manufacturing Management

A central principle of the new manufacturing strategy, sometimes called a manufacturing revolution, is that products must be designed so that they can be built more easily, at lower costs, and of higher quality. The key elements in modern manufacturing strategy include:

- *Simultaneous engineering* where a team including design and manufacturing engineers, marketers, suppliers, product workers, salespeople, and service representatives work together in the same location to design the product and its supporting organizational processes.

- *Reduction of inventories* through the use of new management strategies where inventories are provided just in time for the next step in the manufacturing process, helping to eliminate costly warehousing and inventory carrying costs.

- *Flexible manufacturing systems* so that one assembly facility can make many different kinds of products as the market shifts. Many times entire families of products—or even a unique item—can be made on the same production line.

- *Production and quality teams* which empower employees to become responsible for how the work is done—teams of production workers cooperate through peer groups to set and attain high quality and productivity effort from their colleagues.

- *First-level supervisors* become less the boss and more a facilitator and coach to provide the resources and culture for the workers to do much of their own planning and control.

- *Empowered workers* who have more authority and accept more responsibility for how the work is done. Workers are often formed into teams but may continue to work alone but with more interface with their peers in doing the jobs.

- *Continuous training* of the work force, particularly the manufacturing people, who are taught to do many different jobs, allowing for the elimination of many different job classification systems. Workers are rewarded for doing the job and for learning new jobs in their work environment.

- *Continuous quest for quality* through the setting of explicit quality objectives, goals, and strategies and the fine tuning of the environment where the competitive products are analyzed through benchmarking techniques to become the "best of the class" in the quality of the products and the processes required to bring the product to the market.

- *Automation* strategies allowing automated tools like pick-and-place robots to do what they do best and people to do what they do best in meeting quality and productivity objectives.

- *Elimination of paperwork* through the judicious use of computers and networks to store and retrieve data and information used in the programming and control of the manufacturing operations.

- *Strategic alliances* with suppliers where long-term contracts are used to bring favored suppliers into the simultaneous engineering process as well as provide just-in-time support of high-quality products as needed without any incoming inspection or storage of components and subsystems.

- *Computerized order entry* systems that enable customer orders to initiate the "pulling" of products through the manufacturing system when a customer order triggers a response back down the line and replacement items are made.

- *Material requirements planning* where information and computer technology combined with the logistics needs of the manufacturing system can be integrated and programmed.

The implementation of improved U.S. manufacturing strategies is challenging for all.

The selection and implementation of appropriate manufacturing systems technologies will continue to become more complex as product-process technologies continue to advance. Since 1981 the National Institute of Standards and Technology (NIST) has operated a laboratory called the Automated Manufacturing Research Facility (AMRF) to conduct research in automated manufacturing equipment and systems, as well as to provide a test bed where researchers can work together on projects of mutual interest, such as advanced manufacturing technologies.

To bring the results of NIST research to American manufacturers, especially small and midsized companies, NIST inaugurated the Manufacturing Technology Centers (MTC) program as charged in the Omnibus Trade and Competitiveness Act of 1988. The objective of this program is to enhance productivity and technological performance in U.S. manufacturing organizations. The premise of the MTC program is that small and midsized manufacturers are limited in their ability to identify and apply advanced manufacturing solutions to their business needs. The MTCs work to improve this situation by assisting in the promotion, assessment, training, and implementation of advanced manufacturing technology.

These MTCs are a form of "shared manufacturing" initiatives and represent a real government support to the improvement of U.S.

manufacturing competitiveness. Much more needs to be done, however, as in continued research.

Research in New Manufacturing Strategy

John Seely Brown, a corporate vice president at Xerox and the director of the Xerox Palo Alto Research Center (PARC), makes the important point that research on new work practices is as important as research on new products.[19] Considering the need for improvement in U.S. manufacturing systems technologies, the point that Brown makes takes on added significance.

Effective development and implementation of new technology demands a clear appreciation bolstered by a viable strategy of the effects of the technology on the other systems of the enterprise. The benefits of technological improvement must concurrently be adjusted to the need for changes in the management, social, cultural, and business systems of the organization. Most of these improvements in the other systems of the business require creative initiatives from managers and workers, the cooperation of all people in the enterprise, and changes in the relationships with customers, suppliers, and other stakeholders of the company. A fundamental cultural and attitudinal shift will be required on the part of everyone. Organizational structure changes will become the norm; manufacturing will continue to be thought of more as a system, with extensive integration, cooperation, and coordination between functions to achieve competitive goals. Workers will have more authority, responsibility, and greater job security, and will be more valuable, active participants in the manufacturing system. But the changes will not come about without resistance, as vested interests—both managers and workers—see their power in the traditional practices and organizational structures wane. Manufacturing will provide fewer job opportunities. Those opportunities that survive will require fewer unskilled and semiskilled workers, but the jobs that survive and are created in the future will be more challenging and rewarding.

Local, regional, and national government policymakers will need to recognize that the continued performance of manufacturing at any level to maintain global competitiveness will need to have help. These policymakers will have to change their expectations of manufacturing, and encourage the general public to adjust their image and expectations of manufacturing.[20]

Cooperation among the players in industry, universities, and the government has greatly facilitated the development and transfer of product manufacturing technology. In the United States, partnership and interaction among these players involved in improving the product-process design capabilities of the American industrial base have diminished to the point where none serves the needs of the others. Nor has the U.S. government recognized the enhancement of engineering design capabilities to be of national importance.[21] In engineering schools the curriculum has focused on a few traditional design procedures rather than on the total product-process design challenge. According to a report by the National Research Council:

> This state of affairs virtually guarantees the continued decline of U.S. competitiveness. To reverse this trend will require a complete rejuvenation of engineering design practice, education, and research, involving intense cooperation among industrial firms, universities, and government.[21]

Changes coming about in the technology and management of manufacturing are without precedents. The central ideas underlying modern global manufacturing are that products and manufacturing processes have to be *developed concurrently, at lower cost, of higher quality, leading to faster commercialization of products and services.*

Concurrency

The concurrent (or simultaneous) development of products and supporting processes is under way in forward-thinking manufacturing establishments. Some examples follow:

- At Hewlett-Packard the objective is to fashion a link between engineering and manufacturing strong enough that the two organizations literally lose their independent look and feel. HP's rule of thumb: If you walk into a company and can distinguish engineering from manufacturing, something is wrong. Engineering should be integrative—the functional barriers should be destroyed which separate design and manufacturing engineering.[22]

- In the development of the Saturn automobile GM's union-management team conducted benchmarking studies of nine GM plants, and 60 other companies agreed that the development of the Saturn automobile would be possible with two "ifs": First, *if* their conflict resolution process was adopted, and second, *if* technology and resources were properly integrated. To satisfy the first if, all key stakeholders would have to participate in the process and have access to all information. The people using the manufacturing tooling and equipment would be involved in their layout and design. This would lead to the use of a product-process design team to concurrently develop the car design.

Manufacturing is preceded by effective and accurate design. Engineering design is as well a critical part of the new product realization process. It is estimated that 70 percent or more of the life cycle cost of a product is determined during design. Global competitors have shown that effective product-process design accomplished through the medium of a product-design team can improve quality, reduce costs, speed time to commercialization, and in the process match a competitor's engineering and capability to global customers' needs. A *Dataquest* study shows that product changes that cost $1000 during the design phase could easily cost $10 million during final production (Ref. 22, p. 34).

One of the key requirements to move toward a world-class manufacturing capability is to understand the need and benefits of concurrently designing the product processes and the need for quickly getting product concepts to the market. Both product and process technology play an important part in world-class manufacturing. But the emphasis cannot be solely on technological solutions—the people, organizations, and cultural considerations are equally if not more important. Technological panaceas don't do the job.

Technological innovations in manufacturing are spreading rapidly, in part because of the growth in research consortia and other forms of strategic alliances. The efficiencies of global communication and transportation networks make it virtually impossible to maintain a technological proprietary advantage. The commercialization of product technology is becoming more dependent on concurrent engineering. The ability to commercialize technology faster than the competitors has become at least as important as the classical sources of advantage such as economies of scale, a skilled work force, proprietary technology, and access to financial resources.

The simple fact is that effective product design and manufacturing know-how are inseparable; both are necessary to produce high-quality products that can be priced competitively. Effective design is a prerequisite for effective manufacturing; quality cannot be manufactured into a product or be tested into a product. It must be designed into it.

Many of the needed manufacturing technology improvements are not available to an important segment of American industry—the small and midsized manufacturers.

The Small and Midsized Manufacturers' Dilemma

The development of strategies by *large* manufacturers to compete more effectively in the global marketplace is under way in many manufacturing enterprises. Resource availability for these enterprises is usually not a problem. Reallocation of existing resources through restructuring, cost cutting, and elimination of products and services that do not provide adequate contribution to profitability are the challenges facing these large companies. *Small* and *midsized* manufacturers have a more serious challenge. Finding adequate resources to learn and adopt new technical and management strategies to compete effectively in the global marketplace is difficult and often impossible for small enterprises. Yet in some countries small manufacturers are thriving.

Manufacturing

Japanese large industrial combines are more like "trading companies" than traditional manufacturers. Rather than design and manufacture their own goods, they actually coordinate a complex design and manufacturing system that involves thousands of smaller companies. The larger companies farm out much of their work to small subcontractors who in turn subcontract to even smaller companies. Small to midsized companies make up more than 99 percent of Japanese industry. Over 75 percent of all registered Japanese companies are capitalized under $70,000. It is evident that the economic success of Japan would not be possible without the support of many small businesses across Japan.[23]

The relative decline of U.S. manufacturing affects the entire manufacturing infrastructure and impacts firms of all sizes. The adoption of advanced production technologies by U.S. manufacturers has been low, particularly for state-of-the-art equipment.

In the United States, this low adoption of advanced production technologies has had a significant impact on the economic health of the approximately 350,000 small manufacturers—those with fewer than 500 employees. Accordingly, the relative productivity and earnings of these small firms have declined during the 1980s. Yet these smaller companies have generated the majority of new jobs created in manufacturing during recent years.[24]

Some believe that the real crime being perpetrated on the American economy is the erosion of our technology base, particularly for small and midsized manufacturers. The term *technology* is being used in a general sense—a technology of marketing, manufacturing, sales, product development, human resources, quality, information systems, vendor management—extending to all the functions of the enterprise. Progress is being made in the United States in improving quality, productivity, and after-sales service, but we have a long way to go—particularly the small and midsized manufacturing firms that have particular challenges in trying to meet global competition. Clearly something needs to be done.

Help Needed

If nothing is done to help small and midsized U.S. manufacturers that major OEMs depend on, what will be the impact of these large companies trying to compete in the global marketplace? Small and midsized manufacturers show limited interest in investing in new manufacturing technology because of the risks and financial implications involved. If help is not forthcoming to these small and midsized manufacturers, the large OEMs will be required to become more dependent on foreign outsourcing, with the consequent risk of loss of competitiveness by all U.S. manufacturers.

When the small and midsized manufacturers provide goods and services to the OEMs, there is a two-way technology transfer advantage. The small firms learn from and teach the larger ones. As the small firms master new technology, it is expected to be shared with their customers. As the use of concurrent engineering spreads, and the small and midsized vendors join the product-design teams organized by the OEMs, a greater flow of two-way technology will result. The ability of the U.S. manufacturing community to create and commercialize innovative products using state-of-the-art manufacturing processes depends greatly on the health of the small and midsized manufacturing community in each industry.

Small and midsized manufacturers employ more than 8 million workers and generate more than half of all manufactured value in the United States. Smaller manufacturers, in general, are technologically backward compared with the large multinational manufacturers to whom they sell components and subassemblies.[25]

Also, too many small and midsized manufacturers lack knowledge about how they contribute to world-class manufacturing. They do not truly appreciate the strategic implications of their pivotal position in helping the OEMs maintain global competency. These small and midsized manufacturers lack adequate information about state-of-the-art manufacturing systems and what such systems can do for them. Most lack the computer literacy that is needed to use programmable automation; nor do they understand the new organizational and management methods that have emerged to support the development and application of world-class manufacturing.

The capacity of the U.S. manufacturing community to develop and commercialize new products and processes will suffer if the small and midsized manufacturers do not modernize. Once the small and midsized manufacturers are provided appropriate manufacturing assistance through a comprehensive national manufacturing policy and are able to master and accommodate new manufacturing systems technology, they will increasingly develop the capacity to respond innovatively as suppliers to the product-process requirements of their OEMs. Since technology transfer tends to go both ways by responding innovatively to their OEM's needs, an overall synergistic contribution in their industries should result. The authors believe that manufacturing assistance centers based on the concept of shared manufacturing must be one element in the formulation of a national manufacturing policy.

Shared Manufacturing Systems

Shared manufacturing is defined as *different manufacturers with similar needs sharing modern manufacturing technologies, facilities, equipment, and management systems.* A review of the foreign competition for American manufacturers leads one to the idea that the use of shared manufacturing centers in one form or another is a growing part of the improvement of global manufacturing productivity and quality. The Pacific Rim competitors have brought about the use of shared manufacturing strategies through the government sponsorship of productivity and quality improvement programs. Large-scale productivity and quality-awareness campaigns have been sponsored by governments as well as open and facilitating attitudes toward the transfer of technology from other nations into the Pacific Rim competitors. Japan has provided over $500 million to set up such shared manufacturing capabilities. There is no doubt that such centers have improved the ability of the Japanese to compete in global markets. We believe that the United States needs to provide funding and support to set up a national network of such shared manufacturing centers. High-tech companies are leading the charge for national policies to raise the competitiveness of U.S. companies. One of their recommendations is *increasing efforts to spread advanced manufacturing methods to companies.*[26]

To take full advantage of new technologies and to keep pace with global competitors, companies must invest heavily in capital-intensive equipment that incorporates new and sometimes untested technologies—both at the process and at the system level. While this strategy is certainly effective at the macro level over the long range, it is difficult to implement in small and midsized companies that do not have the financial resources. The situation is further exacerbated because the cost of capital investment in the United States is estimated to be two to three times greater than in many foreign competitors.[27] Organizations such as Centre Technique des Industries Mechaniques (CETIM) in France and the Fraunhofer Institute in Germany (detailed in later chapters) have successfully used shared manufacturing philosophies to aid small and midsized firms. The vision of shared manufacturing is also being realized in the United States, although on a limited basis. According to Deborah L. Wince-Smith, former assistant secretary for technology policy at the U.S. Department of Commerce, a handful of such facilities are up and running and a number of others are into the planning stage.[28]

The concept of shared manufacturing stems from the need for companies to evaluate new processes, new technologies, new designs, and prototypes before incorporating them into their own facilities. This can be implemented in the form of *strategic alliances* between community-sponsored shared manufacturing assistance centers (SMACs) and local manufacturers. The purpose of such a center would be to enable small companies to evaluate new process technologies, new product designs, and logistics and management systems before incorporating the advancements into their own facilities and company strategies. In addition, these SMACs can provide the buffer capacity needed by small manufacturers. The creation of SMACs capable of performing as a common community-shared manufacturing facility can provide the resources for companies that cannot afford the financial and technological risk of developing their own competitive product and process strategies and capabilities.

The 1990s will continue to show both technological and managerial innovations in manufacturing systems. As those innovations continue to be diffused throughout the global manufacturing community, the need for the sharing of manufacturing resources through some form of strategic alliance will become more apparent. Small and midsized manufacturing companies will continue to have financial limitations in the development of new facilities, equipment, and manufacturing management strategies. A general turning to *shared manufacturing* in the global manufacturing community will become more pronounced.

What are the benefits to be expected by a company contemplating participating in a shared manufacturing center? As an assumption, participating in such a center will provide advantages that the typical small and midsized firm would not be able to obtain independently. These advantages include:

- Availability of manufacturing management and technology knowledge that can be obtained at a small percentage of the cost of obtaining assistance independently.

- Elimination of the need to make capital investment for improving state-of-the-art manufacturing systems. By testing out the capital equipment in a shared manufacturing center, the suitability of the equipment can be tested prior to making significant capital investments to own or lease the equipment.

- By building a strategic alliance with a regional shared manufacturing center the small and midsized company has a basis on which to plan for the advancement of manufacturing systems technology in their company. As the company participates in a sharing context with other firms, networks will be built and maintained for the transfer of manufacturing systems technology.

- By entering into a sharing alliance with such centers the companies can learn the benefits of working cooperatively with local firms—even competitors—in doing research, building prototypes, and training the employees and will gain insight into present and expected state of the art in their manufacturing processes.

- Capital equipment, research and development, training, software development, and product technology can all be shared, thus reducing the overall risk to the company.

- Sharing for large companies participating in the facility includes having a place to work with small and midsized companies who are supplying parts and subsystems to the OEM. This sharing away from the OEM's place of business reduces the interference of having several vendors working in the OEM's facility and should simplify the management of the OEM's research and manufacturing organizations.

Without doubt, the United States will be hard-pressed to restore its overall global leadership in manufacturing. The restoration of this leadership will require public investment, private initiatives, and cooperation among many "stakeholders" of U.S. manufacturing competitiveness. We believe that *shared manufacturing* is a proper step toward the restoration of U.S. manufacturing competitiveness.

Conclusion

There is a risk that a lot of manufacturing will be gone from this country by the turn of the century. The current competitive pressures in Europe and the Far East will be joined by the anxious competitors bound to emerge in eastern Europe. How far behind will other countries like Mexico and Canada be when free trade becomes a reality in the Western Hemisphere? What is at stake is our national strength, our pride, and our standard of living. Incentive programs to encourage investment in new technologies will help in finding ways for companies to cooperate with each other in strategic alliances. More favorable legislation and better education in teaching the young generation about manufacturing systems technology will also help. But the bulk of the remedial action to improve America's manufacturing systems capability rests with the manufacturing managers and employees. The buck clearly stops with them.

The decline of U.S. international manufacturing competitiveness has been blamed on many factors, including national fiscal and trade policies, exchange rates, national culture, antiquated manufacturing capabilities, management and accounting practices, unfair foreign trade practices, and the methods of providing venture capital to American manufacturers. A crucial factor that is not often recognized is the quality of cooperation among regional industry, universities, and governments. Another key factor that is often not given its due is the quality of the product-process design strategy used by contemporary organizations. The ability to develop new products using state-of-the-art manufacturing processes which reflect high quality and low costs that meet customers' quality needs is essential to increasing a firm's profitability and strategic survival and growth chances in the global marketplace—this all will lead to improved national competitiveness.

Even if manufacturing in the United States is able to hold its present position, that is not going to be good enough with the growing and spreading competition in the global environment. New technologies have come to the front in manufacturing. We are in a position similar to the farmers in the 1870s—the reaper had been invented, and it was known that it would have some impact on the agricultural industry—but it was not known just how and how far that transformation was going to take place. One thing is certain. We face enormous challenges in marshaling and organizing technology, people, and finances in meeting global competition. The changes that have already started in the manufacturing community are without precedent in the history of the United States. The U.S. manufacturing base has so eroded in some industries that it poses a threat to our national security and to our economic strength. Although the United States still maintains a lead in *inventing* new technologies, too many global competitors are beating us in commercializing new product-process technology, ultimately leading to better performance in the marketplace. It gives little satisfaction that we are good at creating new technologies but that we are not preeminent in managing that technology. Unless we get our act together in better managing manufacturing technology, we will continue to see our manufacturing base erode and our entire economy risk decades of decline.

How tragic, to paraphrase an old saying—for want of effective support of manufacturing systems technology, a national economy was lost! We continue to invent technology faster than we are able to effectively manage it. Our problem is not manufacturing technology alone—it is the strategic management of that technology as well. And small and midsized manufacturers need considerable help. *Shared manufacturing* will help these manufacturers through providing for the cooperative efforts of regional industry, universities, and local, state, and federal government.

References

1. Chase, Richard B., and David A. Garvis, "The Service Factory," *Harvard Business Review*, July–August 1989, pp. 61–62.
2. Kanter, Rosabeth Moss, "Thinking Across Boundaries," *Harvard Business Review*, November–December 1990, pp. 9–10.
3. *Industrial Modernization: An American Imperative,* The National Coalition for Advanced Manufacturing, Washington, D.C., October 1990.
4. Reich, Robert B., "Who Is Them?" *Harvard Business Review*, March–April 1991, pp. 77–88.
5. Ohmae, Kenichi, *The Borderless World—Power and Strategy in the Interlinked Economy,* Harper Business, Harper Collins Publishers, 1990 McKinsey & Company, Inc.
6. Kanter, Rosabeth Moss, "Transcending Business Boundaries: 12,000 World Managers View Change," *Harvard Business Review,* May–June 1991, p. 151.
7. Magnusson, Paul, Commentary, *Business Week,* Apr. 1, 1991, pp. 1–27.
8. Cook, William J., "Ringing in Saturn," *U.S. News & World Report,* Oct. 22, 1990, pp. 51–54.
9. *Made in America III: The Globalization of Manufacturing.* Survey by Coopers & Lybrand, New York.
10. Coleman, John E., *Manufacturing Engineering,* January 1991, p. 4.
11. Pitta, Julie, "The Realist," *Forbes,* May 13, 1991, p. 116.
12. Ingrassia, Paul, "Auto Industry in U.S. Is Sliding Relentlessly into Japanese Hands," *Wall Street Journal,* Feb. 18, 1990.
13. Coleman, John R., Editor-in-Chief, *Manufacturing Engineering,* May 1990, p. 6.
14. Gupta, Udayan, "Tough Times Can Make Strategic Bedfellows—Alliances between Firms Promote Competitive Strengths, Jordan Lewis Says," *Wall Street Journal* (date unknown).
15. Taylor, William, "The Logic of Global Business: An Interview with ABB's Percy Barnevik," *Harvard Business Review,* March–April 1991, pp. 91–105.
16. Hammonds, Keith H., "Corning's Class Act," *Business Week,* May 13, 1991, pp. 68–76.
17. Wysocki, Bernard, Jr., "Canada Suffers Exodus of Jobs, Investment and Shoppers to U.S.," *Wall Street Journal,* June 20, 1991.
18. Blundell, Wm. R. C., "Prescription for the '90s: The Boundaryless Company," *Business Quarterly,* Autumn 1990, pp. 71–73.
19. Brown, John Seely, "Research That Reinvents the Corporation," *Harvard Business Review,* January–February 1991, pp. 102–111.
20. *Toward a New Era in U.S. Manufacturing—The Need for a National Vision,* Manufacturing Studies Board, Commission on Engineering and Technical Systems, National Research Council, National Academy Press, Washington, D.C., 1986, pp. 1–4.

21. *Improving Engineering Design—Designing for Competitive Advantage,* National Research Council, National Academy Press, Washington, DC, 1991, p. 1.
22. "Engineering: Where Competitive Success Begins," *Industry Week,* Nov. 19, 1990, pp. 30–38.
23. Sakai, Kuniyasu, "The Feudal World of Japanese Manufacturing," *Harvard Business Review,* November–December 1990, pp. 38–49.
24. Small Business Administration, *Handbook of Small Business Data,* 1988, p. 225.
25. "Co-op Lets Small Firms Sample High Technology," *The Pittsburgh Press,* Apr. 22, 1990, p. D20.
26. Carey, John, "Will Uncle Sam Be Dragged Kicking and Screaming into the Lab?" *Business Week,* July 15, 1991, pp. 128–129.
27. Sanderson, Susan Walsh, "The Vision of Shared Manufacturing," *Across the Board,* December 1987.
28. Brandt, Ellen, "A Vision of Shared Manufacturing" (interview with Deborah L. Wince-Smith), *Mechanical Engineering,* December 1990, pp. 52–55.

2

Evaluating
the Need for Shared
Manufacturing Systems

Background

Manufacturing firms are under intense global competition with respect to world-class quality, competitive price, just-in-time delivery, and rapid response to changing market needs and new technologies.[1] It is necessary for American manufacturers to have access to the state-of-the-art technology and management tools to be able to regain their competitiveness in the global market. Emphasizing the need for adopting new technology, Hamid Noori[2] writes:

> ...[the] utilization of growth potential of product and process innovation is required to compete successfully in today's dynamic environment. Companies that fail to recognize the potential of advanced technologies will not be able to respond to the changes in the market place and are doomed to failure.

The adoption of new technology, especially in the United States, has been less than satisfactory. Based on a national survey of 1368 manufacturing establishments in the United States, Kelley[3] makes the following observations:

- Less than 11 percent of the total stock of machine tools in use in the industries studied are computer controlled.

- Fifty-three percent of the plants have not installed more than one automated machine that is computer controlled.

- Of the plants that adopted the technology prior to 1982 and were still in business in 1987, one in four have ceased to make any additional investment in new technology.

- Even among plants that have invested in computerized automation in the last 5 years, the use of new technology in production operations is minimal. In these facilities only about one in six machines are computerized.

While U.S. manufacturers are slow in adopting new technology, the Japanese have been very pragmatic. For instance, Japan has 50 percent more flexible manufacturing systems (FMSs) than the United States, and 40 percent more than the United Kingdom, Germany, France, and Italy combined. Approximately 40 percent of the computerized numerically controlled machine tools installed throughout the world have been in Japan, twice the U.S. number. U.S. industry has not yet recognized that the success of the Japanese is a result of their commitment to manufacturing excellence.[4]

Small Manufacturers and Advanced Technology

There are many benefits to small and midsize firms in adopting new technology. Small firms often compete through new products. If small firms are to compete successfully, it is necessary for them to utilize new technologies and to introduce new products faster into the market, given today's shorter product life cycles.

Other benefits of automation to small firms include faster innovation, shorter lead time, the ability to produce a greater variety of products, and higher growth rates.[5] In an interview with Sanderson,[6] Bruce Merrifield, a former Assistant Secretary of Commerce, warns: "Any company that has not, or is not currently, making accelerated investments in either development or adaptation of advanced technology has made a strategic decision to be out of business in 5 to 10 years."

There are approximately 360,000 small manufacturers in the United States. Seventy percent of the component parts used by the large manufacturers come from over 130,000 small firms.[7] They employ more than 8 million workers and generate more than half of all the manufactured value in the United States.[8] According to David Birch, an MIT researcher, small companies of fewer than 100 employees are responsible for as many as 8 out of 10 new jobs. Although small firms are not involved in global markets themselves, they have an important indirect effect on U.S. competitiveness, as suppliers to large manufacturers. Government spending for the assistance of these manufacturers, including federal, state, and local support, is a mere $50 million, reaching only 2 percent of these manufacturers. In contrast, the Congressional Office of Technology

Assessment (OTA) estimates that the Japanese government provides about 20 times more financial aid to small business than the U.S. government does. In 1988 alone, low-cost direct loans to smaller companies from government financial institutions in Japan amounted to more than $27 billion—with loan guarantees providing an additional $56 billion.[9] The relative lack of infrastructure in the United States to support small manufacturers is one reason why they lag behind their counterparts from other industrialized nations. Any strategy to improve a country's manufacturing competitiveness should bring the needs of the small manufacturers into account.

Barriers to New Technology Adoption

A number of factors contribute to the slow adoption of technology. Financial, technical, organizational, managerial, labor, and policy related issues are often identified as being responsible for this tardiness.[10] In spite of the need to implement advanced technology, most firms (especially small and midsized ones) are unable to do so because they lack the necessary financial, technical, and human resources. For instance, a flexible manufacturing system (FMS) can cost from $2 million to almost $50 million and fail to meet the short-term financial rate of return. The cost of capital has risen considerably and the implementation of new technology is often constrained by traditional accounting practices.[11] The cost and availability of capital is often a function of the specific country. For example, the cost of capital in the United States is 2 to 3 times higher than in Japan and Germany.[6] Some Pacific Rim countries like Japan have financial systems that permit a high debt-to-equity ratio that makes it easier for companies to raise capital for new technology implementation.[4]

The implementation of new technology typically entails substantial organizational time and commitment. Even in cases where new technology implementation is successful, the time needed for this technology to accrue economic benefits is often greater than anticipated. For example, FMS implementation often takes twice the expected time.[5] Many companies prefer to avoid risks, believing that if no technology is introduced, there will be no disruption in production. Introduction of new technology without accompanying change in the plant operations does not achieve the desired results.[4,5]

Technology is changing very rapidly, contributing to one more reason why many companies are slow in adopting new technology. Consider the following excerpt:

> The various types of technology used to improve productivity and quality in the early 1960s had an average life cycle of about 10 years.... In

1986, most technology life cycles have been shortened to about two years and are projected to be about six months by the year 2000. The continued shortened life cycle poses a real challenge for organizations that desire to use technology as a mechanism for productivity and quality improvement.[12]

The implication of shorter technology life cycles is that organizations will have a shorter window of opportunity in which to adopt new technology. There will be little room for procrastination and extended feasibility studies. It is becoming increasingly challenging for organizations to keep abreast of changing technology, identify technology most suitable to their needs, and find necessary financial and human resources to buy and implement it in a timely manner.

Surveys conducted by Deloitte and Touche in the United States point to a disturbing trend with respect to new technology implementation. The results reveal a declining interest in new technology. The majority of manufacturers have little or no experience with advanced manufacturing technologies, and only a handful claim to be applying them at the state-of-the-art level. Perhaps the most disturbing trend that survey identified is the decline of manufacturers citing significant benefits from the application of advanced technology.[13]

In order to be able to compete effectively, companies must invest heavily in capital-intensive equipment that incorporates new and sometimes untested technologies. While this strategy has proved to be effective over the long range, companies that do not have large financial resources often find it impossible to implement. One way to help small and midsize manufacturers overcome these barriers is to establish industry-university-community–sponsored networks of *manufacturing assistance centers* (SMACs) based on the concept of *shared manufacturing*. Such facilities would enable small and midsize firms to be able to evaluate in detail new processes, new technology, new equipment designs, manufacturing process prototypes, and supporting logistic and management systems before incorporating them into their own facilities and company strategy.[14] According to Merrifield,[10] the former Assistant Secretary of Commerce, such alliances:

- Multiply the world market potential for a new product, process, or service at less cost to each partner.

- Avoid wasteful redundant activity, pool limited resources and skills, and shorten development times.

- Accelerate diffusion of advanced technology and the formation of new small businesses.

- Allow increased specialization among allied firms.

- Help companies to compete better with vertically integrated and government-subsidized consortia in other countries.

- Help compete with countries that have an advantage of low-cost labor and natural resources.

Thus SMACs based on the concept of shared manufacturing are an important strategy needed to improve the competitiveness of the small and midsized manufacturers in a given region.

Governments in industrialized nations like Germany, England, Italy, and Japan have provided the necessary infrastructure for networks based on shared manufacturing to flourish. For instance, the Japanese government provides half of the $470 million annual budget for a national system of 180 testing and research centers. For a small fee, companies use equipment at the center that they cannot afford to purchase on their own and consult experts about special problems.[9]

The Emilia-Romagna region of north central Italy is another example of successful networking and sharing of resources by small manufacturers. This region has about 90,000 small manufacturing companies, a vast majority with 50 employees or less. The networks are largely the creation of the regional government in collaboration with entrepreneurs and worker unions. The Emilia-Romagna government has helped set up 10 centers for networks throughout the region. One such center, CETIR, does market forecasting and research and provides access to new technologies for about 600 small knitwear companies in the city of Carpi. Through CETIR, these companies have access to advanced technologies and global markets they could never develop on their own.[9] Other examples of shared manufacturing strategy are detailed in later chapters.

Programs for Regional Industrial Development

Over the years, a number of technology assistance initiatives have evolved to provide the impetus needed for industrial growth. These programs differ significantly in terms of their objectives, affiliations, stakeholders, cost of development, size of spatial development, type of industries they serve, and services they provide. Figure 2.1 illustrates a taxonomy of these programs based on size and cost of development continuum.[15] Some of the common forms of regional industrial development programs geared to assist the development and use of science and technology include incubators, innovation centers, shared manufacturing centers, research parks, technology complexes, and technopoleis. A brief description of each of these programs is provided below.

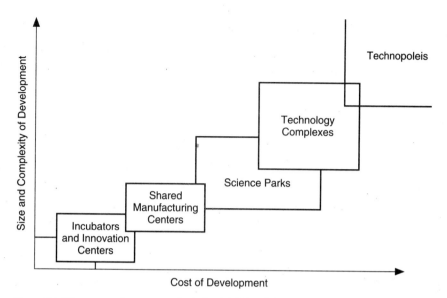

Figure 2.1 Taxonomy of programs for industrial development.

Incubators and innovation centers

The words "incubator," "innovation center," "enterprise center," and "business and technology center" are used interchangeably.[16] To "incubate" is to maintain under prescribed and controlled conditions favorable for hatching or developing. It also means to cause to develop or to give form and substance. Thus a new business incubator seeks to give form and substance to start-up or emerging companies by maintaining controlled conditions for their development and sustenance.

Incubators typically provide four types of support systems: secretarial support, administrative assistance, facilities support, and business expertise.[15,16] They generally consist of a single building or cluster of buildings which may be used to house new and very small firms. Most offer facilities for easy informal contact between entrepreneurs and academic staff from area educational institutions.

Brandt[17] defines four kinds of incubators based on sponsorship, affiliations, and goals: (1) university-based centers, (2) centers sponsored by nonprofit economic development groups or sponsored directly by governments, (3) privately sponsored for-profit centers, and (4) hybrids—the centers that share characteristics of at least two of the other types.

Shared manufacturing systems

Shared manufacturing is defined as the networking of different manufacturers with similar needs sharing modern manufacturing technologies, facilities, equipment, and management systems.[18] It is a strategy that small and midsize manufacturers use to realize the synergistic benefits of sharing resources.

The concept of shared manufacturing assistance centers is a useful new concept that fills the void between the services offered by incubators and the research parks. While the incubators seek to give form and substance to emerging companies, the shared manufacturing centers focus on the needs of the existing mature companies. The objective of these centers is to help small and midsize manufacturers improve their competitiveness by providing them with technical and managerial manufacturing systems support.

Science parks

The terms "science park" and "technology complex" are often used interchangeably. A "park" signifies a single site, whether small or extending to several thousand hectares and accommodating several, perhaps scores or a few hundred buildings, each group of buildings housing separate firms or undertakings. If the park is not a single site but is made up of two or more physically separate blocks, they usually are in close proximity to justify the term "park." The emphasis is on contiguity.[19]

A "complex" is typically more extensive. Here the emphasis is on linkages between the undertakings constituting the complex. The common characteristic is that all these undertakings represent a concentration of activities utilizing high-technology research and development results from or through scientific research or product or process development.

According to one definition, a science park is "an equipped area in the vicinity of public institutions—universities, research agencies—which caters to and promotes the settlement of different users characterized by the activity they are intended to carry on—generally research, development and construction of prototypes."[20]

Complexes and parks may be mutually supportive. The "Cambridge phenomenon" is a good example. This science park in Great Britain was established by Trinity College, as part of the university. Not only has it flourished but many other high-technology organizations have done likewise even though they were not in the park. The whole district has so much momentum in the high-technology sector that other developers have opened up other parks, not necessarily confined to high-technology activities but making some contribution in that direction.[19]

Technopolis

"Polis" is the Greek word for city. Thus "technopolis" implies a technology city. Japan's Tsukuba Science City and Sophia Antipolis in France are two examples of the technopolis concept. The Japanese program for a whole series of "technopoleis" constitutes the largest-scale attempt at the deliberate stimulation of technological advance and its marriage with regional development to be found anywhere. The prevailing philosophy in France also favors a comprehensive approach in which the promotion of high-technology concentrations is considered alongside other aspects of community life.[19]

Some of the common features of these development programs is that they typically deal with high-technology activity and in many cases work closely with academic institutions.

Assessment of benefits

It is difficult to accurately quantify the benefits derived from these programs, since it usually takes many years for benefits to accrue. Most of the initiatives that we might turn to, however, are relatively new, particularly in the area of shared manufacturing. A second problem relates to the criteria adopted as indicators of success since the objectives pursued are varied. Promoters of shared manufacturing may use the objective of regional industrial development and focus on improving the economic performance of a given region. On the other hand, the objectives may be limited to financial rewards. Other objectives include upgrading technology standards, raising the skill levels within a region, the creation of new jobs, etc. There may also be other objectives that are hard to quantify, such as improvement in working conditions.

Indicators that can be used to evaluate the benefits of these centers include the number of new enterprises opened, employment provided, infusion of high-technology employment, etc.

Historical Perspectives of Shared Manufacturing Concepts

Shared resources are common in the field of computers, libraries, and banking. Also, in the medical field, hospitals have been involved in "hospital alliances" since the seventies. These alliances exemplify organizational strategies that involve cooperation among organizations rather than competition. Such strategies are necessitated by the organizational need to secure access to critical resources, and to enable survival. Alliances enable individual firms to band together, act as one, and thus increase their power in exchanges with suppliers of valued resources.[21]

Spurred by increasing international competition, the rising costs of advanced research, the need to leverage scarce scientific and technical talent, and the desire to share the risk associated with technology generation and commercialization, high-technology firms have begun to join hands in cooperative research activities. The terms "research joint ventures (RJVs)," "cooperative research ventures (CRVs)," and "R&D consortia" are commonly used to describe the various forms of cooperative research activity. Since the passage of the National Cooperation Research Act (NCRA) in October 1984, 137 R&D consortia have filed with the U.S. Department of Justice.[22]

The concept of shared manufacturing, however, is still in its inception. Lieberman[7] outlines some of the benefits of such centers in testimony before the United States House of Representatives Subcommittee on Exports, Tax Policy and Special Problems, Committee on Small Business, as follows:

> Shared Flexible Computer Integrated Manufacturing Centers can provide the following benefits to the small firms: They provide immediate competitive manufacturing capability with no large up-front costs; they significantly increase productivity; they substantially increase quality, reducing major costs of rejects and rework; they facilitate the introduction of new products, including just enough units for testing; they allow the continuous adaptation to changing requirements for products that otherwise would require major retooling and down time; they allow the rapid entry into new markets through low cost, high quality, state-of-the-art manufacturing for new products; they can lengthen the time before a plant becomes obsolete, thereby increasing the calculated return on investment; they can enable a company to shift quickly to making products which are experiencing increases in demand, and away from products that are declining in demand.

The concept of shared manufacturing has been widely employed in Europe, especially in northern Italy and western Germany.[8,9] Currently in the United States, six shared facilities of this type are already operating, one each in Maryland, Massachusetts, Ohio, and West Virginia, and two in Pennsylvania. Seventeen more in 15 different states are in the planning stage. By some estimates there could be as many as 200 shared manufacturing centers operating within the decade.[17] Many of these will work in conjunction with universities where they can teach engineers, technicians, and business school students.

There is a considerable interest in the whole area of shared manufacturing centers—what their objectives are, how they are set up, what costs are involved, who would typically participate, their effectiveness, along with other aspects of these centers.

Methodology for Needs Assessment

In order to successfully develop a shared manufacturing facility, the needs of potential customers must be taken into account. The manufacturing industry comprises widely different companies (or segments) that can be classified on the basis of process technology, plant layout, manufacturing flow type, product type, product variety, etc. Each of these segments may have different needs. It is probably not possible for a single shared facility to cater to all the needs of all manufacturing segments. Therefore, a methodology is needed to clearly identify the market segment that will benefit the most from such a facility and in turn show the most interest in participating in such a facility. A model methodology based on the concept of market segmentation is presented in Fig. 2.2.

This model was used in a study conducted by the authors in southwestern Pennsylvania in 1990. The implementation of this model in the study is described in detail in the case presented below.

The Pittsburgh Study

A model for the development of a shared manufacturing facility is illustrated through a case study of the manufacturing community in the Pittsburgh metropolitan area in the northeastern part of the United States. The resources used and the methodology employed here can serve as the basis for further studies both within and outside the United States.

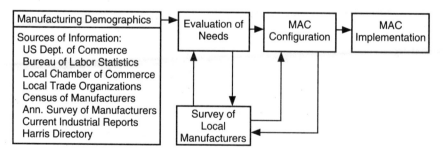

Figure 2.2 Stages of development of a manufacturing assistance center.

Evaluation of area
manufacturing demographics

A manufacturing demographic study provides insight into the types of industries that show the greatest potential for a SMAC and the kinds of SMAC resources and programs that will be required. A good starting point for a demographics study is any local library that serves as a federal depository. U.S. Department of Commerce reports available at the federal depository are a source of information on the industrial composition of a particular area. Several other suggested starting points include the following reports: The *Census of Manufacturers*—a multiple-volume publication that comes out quinquennially providing comparative statistics on a variety of areas; the *Annual Survey of Manufacturers*—a single volume published annually akin to the *Census of Manufacturers* that provides operational statistics; and *Current Industrial Reports*—a publication that discusses market, manufacturing, and policy issues as they relate to specific industries.

Sources from local government agencies are also useful in building a demographic knowledge base. In the current study, these included the annual report from the state Department of Labor and Industry,[23] a special report on manufacturing trends published by the Urban Redevelopment Authority of the City of Pittsburgh,[24] and conference proceedings from the Allegheny County Department of Development.[25]

Though the above sources are informative, they are often outdated. To collect current data, the authors recommend that articles from the daily newspaper, local business newspaper, and local business magazines be reviewed. These indicate the directions being taken by the local economy and its industrial base. Additional sources are periodic employment reports published by state and local government bureaus on industry, labor, and trade. These reports are often printed monthly and track the employment levels for industrial and service sectors. They provide a short synopsis of the employment levels for various industrial sectors while making employment predictions. A series of Labor Market Letters are published monthly by various state departments of industry and trade. For example, a total of 15 Labor Market Letters are published in the state of Pennsylvania alone.

Other sources of information include local chambers of commerce and state industrial directories. In this study, the *Industrial Redliner Report*,[26] published by the Greater Pittsburgh Chamber of Commerce, was used as a primary source of information in developing a database of Greater Pittsburgh area (GPA) manufacturers. Private publishing houses also market statewide manufacturing directories. For example, the Harris Publishing Company publishes the *Harris Pennsylvania Industrial Directory*.[27] Information collected from these directories is company-specific, although the *Harris Industrial Directory* provides summary statistics for individual industry sectors.

Professional associations and government offices are also very useful sources of information. These groups often have membership directories, periodic newsletters, and magazines. They can be very useful in obtaining data on the specific manufacturing segment they represent. Information on associations can be obtained from the *Encyclopedia of Associations,* which lists both local and national associations in the United States. The local government bureau on labor, industry, and trade also maintains such information. For this study, our interactions with the Ben Franklin Technology Center of Western Pennsylvania, Allegheny County Industrial Development Authority, Southwestern Pennsylvania Industrial Resource Center (SPIRC), the Smaller Manufacturers Council, the Pittsburgh High Technology Council, and others proved to be valuable.

Manufacturing demographics of the GPA

We discuss here the industrial demographics of a seven-county region surrounding the city of Pittsburgh area, which is referred to as GPA in this report. The counties incorporated in the GPA include Allegheny (A), Armstrong (B), Beaver (C), Butler (D), Fayette (E), Washington (F), and Westmoreland (G). The regions covered by the study are shown in Fig. 2.3. This seven-county region is a vital part of Pennsylvania, serving as the economic center for western Pennsylvania and the tristate region comprising Ohio, Pennsylvania, and West Virginia. The hub of this economic activity is the city of Pittsburgh, which has a population of over 500,000. The entire GPA has a population of 2,630,600. Many other important municipalities are situated within this seven-county region including the municipalities of Beaver, Butler, Latrobe, Monroeville, and Washington.

Data presented here are at both the individual county and GPA levels. The focus, however, is on the GPA as a whole. The analysis addresses industrial composition through the categories of number of firms per industry, number employed per industry, average firm size per industry, and variations in these categories between 1985 and 1989.

Sources for the demographic data include the *1989 Harris Pennsylvania Industrial Directory* and reports from the Pennsylvania Department of Industry and Trade, Allegheny County, and the Urban Redevelopment Authority. The data for the figures in this chapter are derived from these sources.

Traditionally, the area has been associated with durable goods manufacturing. Today, over 70 percent of manufacturing employment

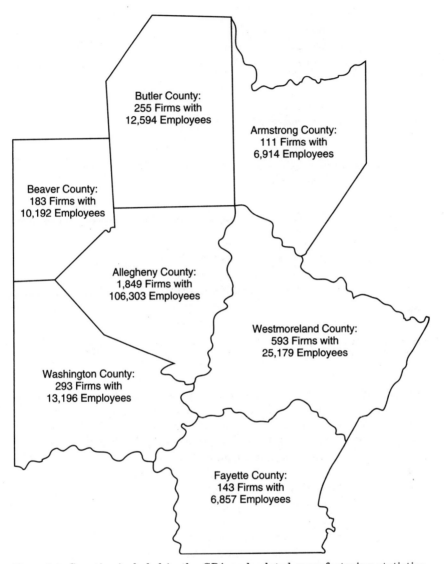

Figure 2.3 Counties included in the GPA and related manufacturing statistics. (Sources: *Industrial Redliner Report* and *1989 Harris Pennsylvania Industrial Directory*.)

is in durable goods manufacturing. The industrial sectors that comprise the majority of this employment are in primary metals, fabricated metals, and industrial machinery, Standard Industrial Classification (SIC) codes 33, 34, and 35, respectively. Over 65 percent of nondurable goods manufacturing is comprised of the industries of chemical products, food products, and printing and publishing.

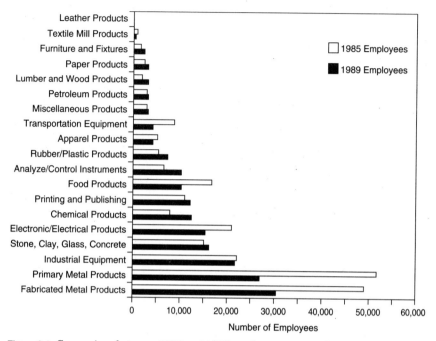

Figure 2.4 Comparison between 1985 and 1989 employment per industry in the Greater Pittsburgh area.

In durable goods manufacturing, the decreases in manufacturing employment experienced during the recessions of the 1970s and early 1980s have continued to the present time. Between 1985 and 1989, employment in the durable goods sector dropped 25 percent. In contrast, employment in the nondurable goods sector rose 3 percent. The industries showing severe decreases were primary metals (−47 percent) and fabricated metals (−37 percent). Figure 2.4 represents the change in manufacturing employment per industry between the years 1985 and 1989.

An interesting phenomenon, however, was that although manufacturing employment had declined, the number of establishments increased. In fact, during the period between 1985 and 1989, the number of manufacturing establishments increased 45 percent. Separately, the durable goods sector showed an increase of 39 percent; nondurable goods showed an increase of 56 percent. The industry exhibiting the greatest growth in establishments was printing and publishing. The next two industries showing the greatest growth were fabricated metals and industrial machinery. The remaining industries had growth equal to or under 100 establishments. Only the textile mill products industry exhibited a decrease in the number

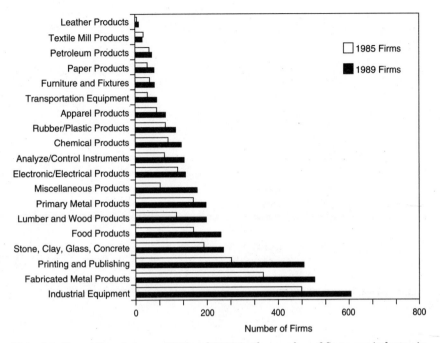

Figure 2.5 Comparison between 1985 and 1989 in the number of firms per industry in the Greater Pittsburgh area.

of establishments (−3 firms). Figure 2.5 gives a comparison between 1985 and 1989 in the number of establishments in the GPA.

With manufacturing employment decreasing in conjunction with the rise in the number of manufacturing establishments, the average size of an establishment (employees per establishment) has decreased. The durable goods sector showed the greatest reduction, with an average employee reduction of 46 percent. The nondurable goods sector reduced 33 percent. The two industries with reductions of over 100 employees were both from the durable goods sector—primary metals and transportation equipment. Figure 2.6 compares the size of firms in 1985 to firms in 1989.

GPA establishments

In 1989, a total of 3427 manufacturing establishments were located in the GPA. The majority of these establishments (2153 firms) were associated with durable goods (Fig. 2.7). The remaining 1274 firms were nondurable goods establishments.

Within the durable goods sector, over half of the establishments were from the primary metals and fabricated metals industries. Food products and printing and publishing made up over half of non-

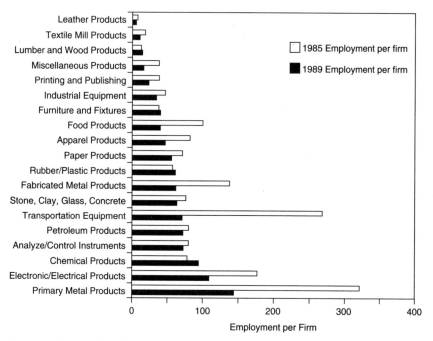

Figure 2.6 Comparison between 1985 and 1989 in the firm size per industry in the Greater Pittsburgh area.

durable goods manufacturers. Overall, the top three industries with respect to number of establishments were fabricated metals (605 firms), primary metals (497 firms), and printing and publishing (466 firms). The remaining industries were under 300 establishments. Figure 2.8 presents GPA composition with regard to number of establishments per industry.

GPA employment

GPA employment in 1989 were estimated at 181,235, with 73 percent of this figure in durable goods manufacturing and 27 percent in nondurable goods manufacturing. The three industries of primary metals, fabricated metals, and industrial machinery accounted for 60 percent of the number employed in durable goods. The three industries of food products, printing and publishing, and chemical products comprised 69 percent of those employed in nondurable goods. Figure 2.9 shows GPA employment composition by industry.

Counties within the GPA

The GPA is comprised of the seven counties of Allegheny, Armstrong, Beaver, Butler, Fayette, Washington, and Westmoreland. Allegheny

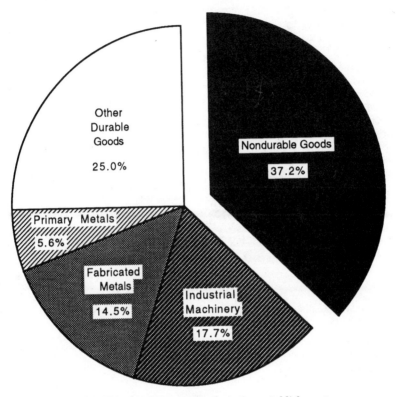

Figure 2.7 Profile of Pittsburgh area manufacturing establishments.

County is the focal point of the region because the city of Pittsburgh is located within that county. Accordingly, Allegheny County has the highest figures for manufacturing establishments and employment among the seven counties.

Between 1985 and 1989, all counties exhibited increases in the number of manufacturing companies, with Allegheny County showing the greatest growth (+610 firms). Figure 2.10 represents the percent change in number of establishments by county. Armstrong and Fayette counties experienced the greatest growth in manufacturing employment. In fact, Armstrong County employment more than doubled between 1985 and 1989. The remaining counties, however, all experienced losses. Allegheny County suffered the greatest numerical unemployment but in terms of percentages, Beaver lost 70 percent of its manufacturing work force. Figures 2.11 and 2.12 show percent changes for manufacturing employment and size of establishment by county between 1985 and 1989.

The conclusions drawn from the demographic study can be summarized as follows:

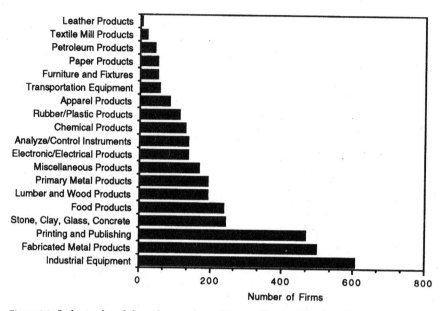

Figure 2.8 Industry breakdown by number of firms—Greater Pittsburgh area.

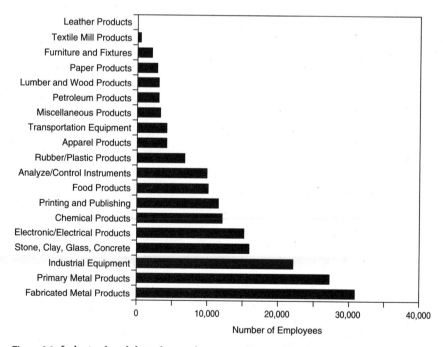

Figure 2.9 Industry breakdown by employment—Greater Pittsburgh area.

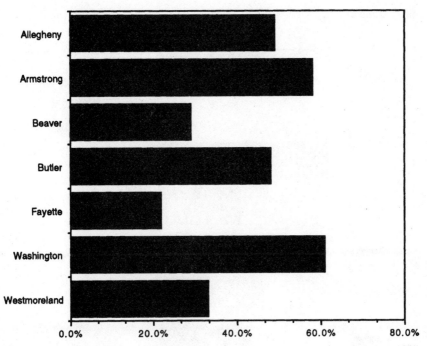

Figure 2.10 Percent change in the number of establishments per county between 1985 and 1989.

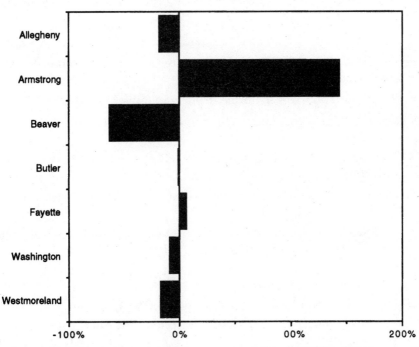

Figure 2.11 Percent change in employment per county between 1985 and 1989.

47

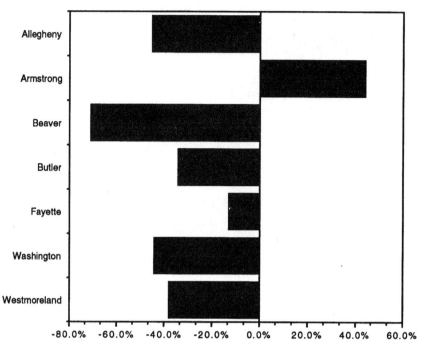

Figure 2.12 Percent change in number of employees per establishment per county between 1985 and 1989.

- The GPA serves as the economic center for western Pennsylvania and the surrounding area.
- The majority of GPA manufacturing is in durable goods.
- Manufacturing employment in the GPA decreased between 1985 and 1989.
- The number of establishments in the GPA increased between 1985 and 1989.
- The average size of an establishment in the GPA decreased between 1985 and 1989.
- Allegheny County has the greatest number of establishments and the highest employment in the GPA.
- All seven counties within the GPA showed an increase in the number of establishments between 1985 and 1989.
- Armstrong and Fayette counties showed an increase in employment between 1985 and 1989; employment decreased in the remaining five counties.

- Armstrong County showed an increase in the size of establishments between 1985 and 1989; all other counties experienced a decrease.

The following section discusses how the demographics relate to the area's need for a SMAC.

Implications of Demographics for Shared Manufacturing

Research has suggested that smaller manufacturing firms do not pursue research and development activities relating to either the product or the process. The rationale is that smaller manufacturers do not have the capital resources to sustain such activities. Although there are exceptions, it is conceivable that the smaller firms would have difficulty in establishing and maintaining research and development facilities as compared with larger companies. With growing global competition, research and development—specifically in product-process development cycle time—has become critical for success.

This study has shown that there are a growing number of manufacturing establishments in the GPA. However, on the average such establishments are smaller in size in comparison to similar firms in 1985. The durable goods sector, which comprises 73 percent of manufacturing employment, has shown significant decreases in the establishment size, dropping from 115 employees per firm in 1985 to 62 employees per firm in 1989. With the size of these firms decreasing, it is apparent that it would be in their best interests to have a SMAC they could use for product-process design and development, buffer capacity, and employee training.

The purpose of the SMAC would be for research and development activities regarding the product and/or process. Such activities could be shared manufacturing or the showcasing of new equipment and methodologies. Among the other activities would be the training of employees and students, for it follows that if firms were to have difficulty sustaining R&D activities, there would also be limited resources (time and capital) to perform training activities. As equipment becomes more sophisticated and computer-integrated, the need for employee training becomes paramount. The center could alleviate the training burden facing smaller manufacturers in the 1990s.

The initial industrial focus of the center should be on the durable goods industries. Expansion into other industries may prove viable in the future. The variety in nondurable goods manufacturing would make it difficult to establish a general-purpose center. It would be especially difficult to find common manufacturing aspects among such varied products as chemicals, textiles, apparel, food, and wood. This is both a result of the majority of establishments and employment being in the durable goods sector and the belief that a center in durable goods manufacturing could cover a greater degree of industries. In particular, metal manufacturing is directly relevant to the industries of industrial and commercial machinery, electronic and electrical products, transportation equipment, and instruments as well as primary metals and fabricated metals.

References

1. U.S. Department of Commerce, "Flexible Computer Integrated Manufacturing and the Ability to Compete in Global Markets," Communication from the Office of Under Secretary for Technology, 1984.
2. Noori, Hamid, *Managing the Dynamics of New Technology: Issues in Manufacturing Management,* Prentice-Hall, Englewood Cliffs, NJ, 1990.
3. Kelley, Maryellen R., and Harvey Brooks, *The State of Computerized Automation in U.S. Manufacturing,* Final Report for NSF Grant SES 8520174 and Office of Technology Assessment of the U.S. Congress Contract 633-2470-0, October 1988, p. 2.
4. Shuman, Larry, *Toward the Realization of the Factory of the Future,* The Institute for Strategic Economics and Industrial Vulnerability, Pittsburgh, Occasional Papers, 1986.
5. Meredith, Jack, "The Strategic Advantages of New Manufacturing Technologies for Small Firms," *Strategic Management Journal,* vol. 8, 1987, pp. 249–258.
6. Sanderson, Susan Walsh, "The Vision of Shared Manufacturing," *Across the Board,* December 1987, pp. 9–11.
7. U.S. Department of Commerce, Testimony of Mark Lieberman before the Subcommittee on Exports, Tax Policy, and Special Problems of the Committee on Small Business, House of Representatives, *Critical Issues Facing Small American Manufacturers,* Government Printing Office, Serial 101-33, Washington, 1990, pp. 4–8.
8. Goozner, Merril, "Manufacturers Stand United: Small Firms Share Tools, Expand Abilities in Co-op," *Chicago Tribune,* Apr. 9, 1990.
9. Howard, Robert, "Can Small Business Help Countries Compete?" *Harvard Business Review,* November–December 1990, pp. 88–103.
10. Merrifield, Bruce, "Strategic Alliances in the Global Market Place," *Research-Technology Management,* January–February 1989.
11. National Coalition for Advanced Manufacturing, "Industrial Modernization: An American Imperative," A NAFCAM white paper, October 1990.
12. Edosomwan, J. A., "Productivity and Quality Management—A Challenge in the Year 2000," 1986 Fall Industrial Engineering Conference Proceedings, Dec. 7–10, Boston, pp. 263–267.
13. Giffy, Craig A., Aleda V. Roth, and Gregory M. Seal, "Survey Shows Priorities Are Quality, Workers and Mature Technologies," *CIM Review,* Fall 1990, pp. 5–15.
14. Cleland, D. I., B. Bidanda, S. R. Dharwadkar, K. Kahn, and C. A. Mullins, *U-PARC Flexible Manufacturing Facility,* Final Report for EDA Grant 01-29-03001, Department of Industrial Engineering, University of Pittsburgh, September 1990.
15. Dharwadkar, Shriram R., *Model for the Development of Shared Manufacturing Assistance Centers,* Dissertation Proposal, Industrial Engineering Department, University of Pittsburgh, Pittsburgh, July 1991.
16. Smilor, Raymond W., "Managing the Incubator System: Critical Success Factors to Accelerate New Company Development," *IEEE Transactions on Engineering Management,* vol. EM-34, no. 3, August 1987, pp. 146–155.
17. Brandt, Ellen, "A Vision of Shared Manufacturing," interview with Deborah L. Wince-Smith, *Mechanical Engineering,* December 1990, pp. 52–55.

18. Bidanda, B., D. I. Cleland, and S. R. Dharwadkar, "Framework for the Design of Manufacturing Assistance Centers," Working Paper, Industrial Engineering Department, University of Pittsburgh, July 1990.
19. Organization for Economic Co-operation and Development, *Science Parks and Technology Complexes in Relation to Regional Development,* Paris, OECD, April 1987.
20. Sunman, Hilary, *The Economics of Technology Change—The European Experience—France and Her Technopoles,* Great Britain, CSP Economic Publications, Ltd., 1986.
21. Zuckerman, Howard S., and Thomas A. D'Anno, "Hospital Alliances: Cooperative Strategy in a Competitive Environment," *Health Care Management Review,* vol. 15, no. 2, pp. 21–30.
22. Smilor, Raymond W., and David Gibson, "Technology Transfer in Multi-Organizational Environments: The Case of R&D Consortia," *IEEE Transactions on Engineering Management,* vol. 38, no. 1, February 1991, pp. 3–13.
23. Commonwealth of Pennsylvania, *Annual Planning Information Report for Pittsburgh PMSA,* Bureau of Research and Statistics, Department of Labor and Industry, Fall 1988.
24. Urban Redevelopment Authority of Pittsburgh, *Manufacturing Trends in Pittsburgh—1980 through 1988,* August 1989.
25. Allegheny Conference on Community Development, "A Strategy for Growth: An Economic Development Program for the Pittsburgh Region," Pittsburgh, 1984.
26. Industrial Map Company, *Industrial Redliner Report,* 1987–1988 edition, Industrial Map Co., Inc., Kentucky, 1987.
27. Fran Segulin (ed.), *1989 Harris Pennsylvania Industrial Directory,* Harris Publishing Co., Ohio, 1989.

3

Configuring
Shared Manufacturing
Assistance Centers

Introduction

Since the development of shared manufacturing assistance centers
(SMACs) involves substantial initial investment, good customer
response is essential for their sustenance and survival. Many such
centers in the United States are supported by public funds in the
early years of their existence and hope to be self-sustaining in 5 to 6
years. Thus there is a considerable interest in identifying the potential users, their technology needs, and ways to configure SMACs that
can best meet the needs of the potential users.

This chapter demonstrates the use of a project life cycle approach
in the development of SMACs with the help of a case study in a large
metropolitan area in the northeastern part of the United States.
Particular emphasis is placed on the necessity of market needs
assessment survey and involvement of potential users in configuring
the center.

SMAC Project: A Life Cycle Approach

The success of SMAC projects depends on how well critical project
parameters such as cost, quality, and technical performance are
attained. We see SMAC projects as going through several different
life cycles characterized by distinct work packages and formal decision points to decide whether to continue with the project or termi-
nate the project depending on the performance in previous phases.
Different authors identify three to seven project life cycle phases with

various terminologies to describe each phase.[1-3] There is a general consensus, however, on the utility of the project life cycle approach and recognition of the fact that each phase is characterized by distinct work packages requiring varying levels of effort. Adams and Brandt describe four project phases: conceptual phase, planning phase, execution phase, and termination phase.[1] Cooper details the activities necessary for new product development and divides them into seven distinct stages.[2] These are: (1) recognition of need, (2) preliminary assessment, (3) concept development, (4) development, (5) testing, (6) trial, and (7) launch. The project is terminated and responsibilities transferred to line authorities once the product is launched. Each stage in Cooper's model consists of several activities and a decision system in place to evaluate further development decisions at each stage. Cooper's model was found to be appropriate for application to implementation of SMACs because of its recognition of the life cycle phases and emphasis on performance evaluation at the end of each phase.

Pittsburgh Study

A case study that uses a modified version of Cooper's model for the development of a SMAC is depicted in Fig. 3.1. The case study illustrates the various stages and the activities conducted at each stage in the development of a SMAC in a large metropolitan area in the northeastern part of the United States.

Recognition of need

The principal motivation for the project came from two primary sources: the needs of the local manufacturing establishments, and the educational curriculum at a large area university. In many interactions with local small and midsized manufacturing establishments, it became clear to the authors that many small and medium-sized companies needed a greater degree of technical and managerial assistance than was currently available to them because of their limited resources.

Concurrently, it became clear that existing curricula at the university, while considered progressive, were not adequately supported by manufacturing facilities in which to conduct classes and do research in an automated factory environment.

Funding to conduct the technical and marketing feasibility study to determine the need for a SMAC and the willingness of local companies to support such a facility came from the local government Industrial Development Authority. In addition, modest funding

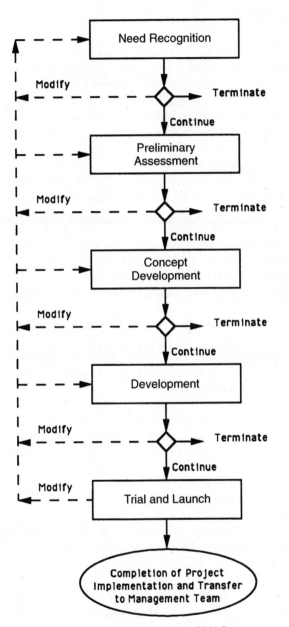

Figure 3.1 Developmental stages in a SMAC.

was also obtained from professional and trade organizations, dedicated to the areas economic development. The study area consisted of the seven-county region contiguous to the proposed location of the SMAC.

Preliminary assessment—selection of market segment

The successful development of SMACs requires careful attention to the needs of the potential customers. The industrial market, however, is made up of different segments with vastly different needs with respect to services and technology. It is impossible for a single SMAC to serve all the industrial segments effectively. Therefore, a methodology is needed to clearly identify the market segment that will have the most interest in the center, so that it will be designed to best meet the needs of this market segment.

Segmentation is the process of separating a market into groups of customers, prospective customers (prospects), or buying situations such that the members of each resulting group are more like the other members of that group than like members of other segments.[4,5] The objective is to divide the markets into groups of potential customers with similar characteristics who are more likely to have similar needs. The segmentation of the market will facilitate the development of a deeper understanding of the needs of the potential customers and help serve them better. It can serve as a basis for developing strategies, plans, and programs for the SMAC that will efficiently meet customer needs.

Bond used the concept of market segmentation in defining the market for science parks.[6] In terms of potential science park occupants, he identifies different market segments based on size, scope, and affiliation, such as start-up companies, existing small and medium companies, small units of large companies, major units of large companies, and noncommercial research institutes. However, in manufacturing, the technology needs differ vastly across the products and manufacturing processes.

The primary market segment for a SMAC can be selected by considering the following: (1) area industrial demographics, (2) expert opinion, and (3) strengths and weaknesses of the promoter of the center. A good match between the strengths of the promoter and the potential needs of the selected market segment is a precursor for the development of a successful center.

Area industrial demographics.   The major thrust of the industrial demographic study was to collect published information to assess the existing manufacturing profile of the study area. This enabled the project team to identify the target market segment and develop an appropriate product mix for the SMAC.

A nonintrusive evaluation of the area demographics was conducted by studying literature published by the federal, state, local, and other economic development agencies. Publications of the area Chamber of

Commerce served as a primary source of information. Another important source of demographic information included a statewide industrial directory published by a private publisher. The available demographic information was used to assess the employment and manufacturing profile within the study area.

The seven-county region and its communities involved in the study had experienced economic decline, population loss, employment decline, and high unemployment rates since 1980. The basic cause of these dislocations was the decline of steel and heavy manufacturing industries, which have been traditionally the most significant industrial sectors of the region.

In the period since 1980, total manufacturing employment in all seven counties declined sharply, with countywide declines ranging from 26 to 74 percent. A total of 125,875 manufacturing jobs were lost since 1980, representing a loss of 45.6 percent. The largest of these declines occurred in the primary metals industries, followed by the fabricated metals and industrial machinery sectors. Unemployment rates increased in all counties in the period between 1980 and 1985, the primary period of structural decline. Highest unemployment rates were recorded at 14.6 percent.

From a detailed evaluation of the area demographics, the following observations were made:

1. A large fraction (63 percent) of the manufacturing sector was involved in the manufacturing of durable goods. Over half were in the areas of primary metals (SIC* 33), fabricated metals (SIC 34), and industrial machinery (SIC 35). A detailed profile of the manufacturing establishments in the study area is provided in Chap. 2.
2. The manufacturing employment in the study area was estimated at 181,235, with 73 percent of the employment coming from durable goods manufacturing. Over 60 percent of durable goods manufacturing was in the sectors represented by SIC codes 33, 34, and 35.
3. More than 80 percent of these manufacturing establishments could be considered small, employing less than 200 employees.
4. The manufacturing employment in the study area decreased significantly between 1980 and 1989.
5. Average size of the manufacturing establishments declined from 95 to 53 employees between 1985 and 1989. The most significant

---

*Standard Industrial Classification (SIC) is an industrial classification system developed by industry experts under the guidance of the Office of Management and Budget of the U.S. Government. Under this system of classification there are twenty major groups (two-digit SIC), 143 industry groups (three-digit SIC), and approximately 450 industries (four-digit SIC) in durable goods.

reduction was experienced by the primary metals sector (SIC 33), with an average decline of over 100 employees per firm.

6. Unemployment level in six of the seven counties in the study area was above the national average.

Durable goods manufacturing with Standard Industrial Classification (SIC) major codes 33 to 39 (see Table 3.1) within a seven-county area contiguous to Pittsburgh was selected as the primary market segment to be the focus of this study. This decision was based mainly on a detailed industrial demographic analysis of the Greater Pittsburgh area (GPA).* The demographic analysis suggested that durable goods comprise the largest segment of manufacturing in the area and have suffered the greatest decline. The abundance of general economic data on the GPA provided a backdrop for identifying the market segments and formed the basis for the next stage of the project—concept development.

Concept development—market research

The objective of this phase was to better understand the users of the project, market segments that were viable, and specific needs of each market segment. The concept development started with a market research effort to seek answers to these questions.

The first step in the market research effort began with the development of a database, which included information about small and mid-sized manufacturing companies within the study area. Each record in the database included the following fields: company name, address, telephone number, contact person, manufactured product, number of employees, and classification of industry sector in the form of SIC code. The study dealt only with durable goods manufacturing with

TABLE 3.1   SIC Industry Groups Selected as Primary Market Segment

SIC number	Major industry group
33	Primary Metals
34	Fabricated Metals
35	Industrial Machinery
36	Electrical/Electronics
37	Transportation
38	Measurement
39	Other

*Greater Pittsburgh area, as referred to here, consists of Allegheny, Armstrong, Beaver, Butler, Fayette, Washington, and Westmoreland counties.

SIC codes 33 to 39. This database was used to conduct a survey of area manufacturers.

The objectives of the survey were to identify the major forces driving the need for improved manufacturing and to determine what strategies should be used in the design and configuration of a SMAC for the study area. The vehicle for this survey was a three-page questionnaire which was mailed to 527 small and midsized firms in the study area. The survey was developed from the understanding gained from a study of the existing industrial demographics for the Pittsburgh community.

Survey of area manufacturers. A survey that addressed 12 areas designed to assess characteristics of the manufacturers, their needs, and their interest in participating in the proposed center was conducted. The questionnaire elicited the following information:

Age and size of firm

Age of equipment

Type of equipment used

End product

Type of process flow

Type of process

Type of market

Product price

Technologies currently in use

Proposed technologies

Challenges faced by the firm

Interest level in proposed center

A total of 527 questionnaires were mailed out with one follow-up letter for nonrespondents. The overall rate of return was 60 percent. Data from the 314 returned questionnaires were entered into a database, and a manufacturing needs analysis was completed. Almost 80 percent of the respondents expressed an interest for the idea of a manufacturing assistance center. A profile of the favorable responses is discussed below:[7]

1. Businesses at least 15 years old: 69 percent
2. Firms employing fewer than 250 employees: 86 percent
    Firms employing fewer than 100 employees: 69 percent
3. Firms using more than 15-year-old equipment: 41 percent
    Firms using at least 5-year-old equipment: 95 percent

4. Firms belonging to primary metals, fabricated metals, and industrial machinery segments (SIC 33 to 35): 64 percent
5. Firms using a job shop or batch flow: 61 percent. Most reported a combination of processes such as assembly, fabrication, and machining.

Figure 3.2 shows that technologies of interest included such capabilities as personal computers on factory floor, computer-aided engineering, robots, flexible manufacturing cells and systems, and CAD to control machine tools. Respondents identified their major challenges as:

- Quality and cost
- Adapting new technology
- Foreign competition
- Hiring and maintaining skilled work force
- Engineering and manufacturing cycle time
- Continuous improvement

Respondents in the survey felt that they needed a SMAC to provide the opportunity for them to learn and observe capabilities such as

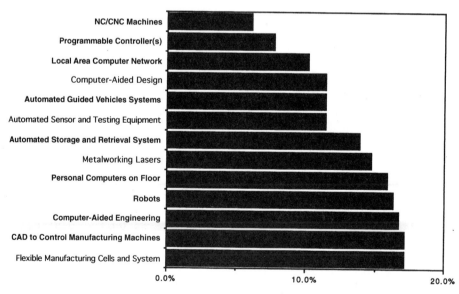

Figure 3.2 Technologies of interest to local manufacturers.

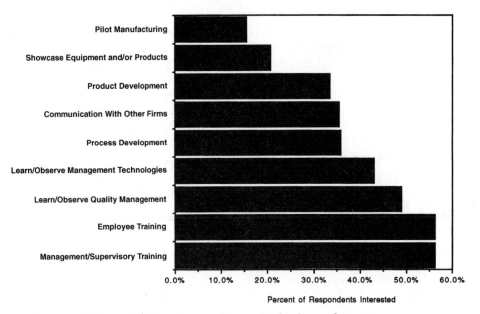

Figure 3.3 Nature of SMAC assistance of interest to local manufacturers.

manufacturing and quality management technologies. Employee and managerial training was also a high-priority need. A complete list of the desired services at a SMAC are detailed in Fig. 3.3.

The strong favorable response to our market survey indicated a need and desire by the area manufacturers in the establishment of a SMAC. Our survey also provided sufficient information on the nature of technologies and services of interest to local manufacturers. Based on this information, a preliminary configuration was developed for the SMAC in the study area. Ten of the favorable respondents were further interviewed to assess the risks involved in the development of the SMAC. Specific questions were asked to seek their likes, dislikes, preferences, reasons for possible discontent, improvement in the design, advice on major considerations, etc. From this valuable input, an improved SMAC concept emerged. This concept could be further refined and validated through focus group processes, and the SMAC configuration should evolve through active interaction with potential users.

Development and testing

The market research carried out in the study area provided the basis for a determination of the market need as well as the specific assistance required by the survey respondents. From the database developed from the market research a preliminary configuration of the SMAC was developed. The set of equipment most suitable for the SMAC was identified as CNC machine tools for traditional machining operations, wire EDM machine, laser metalworking machine tools, automated material handling equipment, robots, metrology equipment, and CAD workstations with solid modeling software.[7]

Human resource development was identified to be an integral part of the SMAC, since the manufacturers in the study area indicated a strong need for education and training. Minilecture modules taught by faculty and industry personnel would allow small and midsize manufacturers to learn and evaluate new technologies such as:

- Metalworking lasers
- Just-in-time manufacturing
- Materials resource planning
- Group technology
- Total quality management
- Computer integrated manufacturing
- CAD modeling
- Simultaneous engineering

The equipment at the SMAC would complement these lectures and give manufacturers firsthand experience in using the equipment and technologies. To meet the needs of manufacturers, the SMAC should focus on the following capabilities:

- Pilot manufacturing
- Product and process development
- Employee and supervisory training
- Study new manufacturing processes and technologies
- Study new management techniques
- Study new quality management technologies
- Showcase new equipment and/or products

An important part of the development and testing phase was the location of funding to design, build, test, and start up the SMAC. The local university in its applied research center has existing facilities that could be retrofitted. Federal and state government agencies, as well as several large corporations and foundations, have provided funding for this important initiative. Machine tool builders and the federal Department of Defense surplus machine tool inventory can be good sources for equipment to outfit the SMAC.

User involvement in configuring the SMAC. The primary objective of the SMACs is to help the manufacturing community improve their competitiveness by providing them with access to state-of-the-art technology. With the enormous growth in automation, there is a wide variety of advanced technology choices that one has to contend with. In order for shared manufacturing centers to succeed, it is necessary that the equipment and the services offered at the center should correspond to the needs of its potential users. Although the preliminary configuration is a direct result of the market needs assessment survey, the final configuration will have to depend on the availability of funds. Therefore, it is necessary to make rational decisions with regard to technology choices. Two important questions pertaining to customer satisfaction need to be addressed:

1. Which are the services (product development, process development, buffer production, training, R&D, etc.) that customers desire and what are the associated relative priorities?

2. What equipment should a center acquire to support the services most desired by the potential customers?

Determination of the optimal configuration for the SMAC is a complex task. The design and configuration of any manufacturing facility involves important choices with respect to many factors such as production capacity, flexibility, and a host of others. The Delphi approach or a focus group approach can be used to assign priorities for the service and equipment needs of the potential users, so that the available resources could be better utilized.

The Delphi technique, developed by Gordon and Helmer, eliminates the inhibition and bandwagon effects often associated with face-to-face interactions by using anonymous questionnaires.[8,9] The responses are processed and sent back to participants. The basic idea is to lead the participants, through a controlled questionnaire, toward a consensus.

Analytical hierarchical process (AHP). The analytical hierarchical process (AHP) can be used to incorporate input from potential customers in making decisions with respect to configuration for SMACs. AHP involves breaking a complex problem into its components and arranging them hierarchically. Using the value judgments assigned to the components, AHP then determines which components of the problem have the highest priority.[10] There have been a number of applications of AHP to decisions relating to technology evaluation and selection.[11-14]

The steps for using AHP in multicriteria decision making are briefly outlined below:

Step 1:   The first step involves defining the decision problem in terms of a hierarchical structure. The overall objective of the problem, which will be the "mission" or "focus," will form the top level of the hierarchy. The lowest level consists of the different alternatives to be considered. The levels in between consist of the various attributes and subattributes affecting the decision problem. The top level will consist of only one element, and the subsequent levels may contain more than one element, preferably under nine.

The hierarchy should be constructed such that elements at a given level are of the same order of magnitude and must be capable of relating to some or all elements of the next higher level.

Step 2:   Make pairwise comparisons by comparing the relative contribution of each element in a given level with respect to a specific element in the immediately higher level. The degree of preference in each pairwise comparison is quantified on a scale of 1 to 9 and tabulated in a matrix form.

The AHP scale for making pairwise comparisons is presented below:

Scale	Definition
1	Equally preferred
3	Moderately preferred
5	Strongly preferred
7	Very strongly preferred
9	Absolutely preferred
2,4,6,8	Compromise between two odd levels

Negative preferences are assigned reciprocals of the above scale.

Step 3:   Obtain the relative weights or priorities of each element in a level. The relative weights are computed as elements of the normalized eigenvector associated with the largest eigenvalue of the comparison matrix. Standard computer programs are available to make these computations, once the comparison matrix is defined. This process is repeated for all levels.

Step 4:   Compute the products of relative weights of all segments in each path from the top of the hierarchy to a given alternative in the lowest level. The sum of these products for all possible paths gives the relative weight (priority) of that alternative.

Since the pairwise comparisons are subjective, there is potential for inconsistencies in the evaluator's judgments. To check for inconsistencies, Saaty [10] suggests using an approximate mathematical indicator called the *consistency ratio* (CR). As a rule of thumb, a consistency ratio of less than 0.1 is considered acceptable. Otherwise, it is recommended that the inconsistencies be resolved by improving the quality of pairwise comparisons. This may involve rephrasing questions, and in some cases restructuring the problem.

AHP application to Pittsburgh study.   The focus of the multicriteria decision problem in the Pittsburgh study was to configure and equip the SMAC that would best serve its potential users. The subjects who participated in this exercise were the most likely users of the SMAC as identified by an in-depth market survey explained earlier.

A four-level hierarchical structure shown in Fig. 3.4 was developed with input from the potential users of the facility. A brief description of the hierarchical levels and the elements is provided below:

Level 1:   This level is the focus of the decision problem. The success of the SMACs depends on how well the facility is designed to meet the needs of its potential users. Thus the focus of the problem is to establish a SMAC with services and technologies that are most preferred by the potential users.

Level 2:   This level represents the different attributes of the SMAC of interest to the potential users. Five attributes—cost, quality, delivery schedule, flexibility, and technology transfer—were identified as having influence over the focus of the SMAC.

Level 3:   This level lists four major services that the SMAC could offer in support of the elements in the next higher level. These services include research, production, technical and managerial consulting, and education and training.

Level 4:   This level lists the equipment alternatives being considered for the SMAC. The elements in this level are the equipment alternatives identified based on the market needs assessment survey.

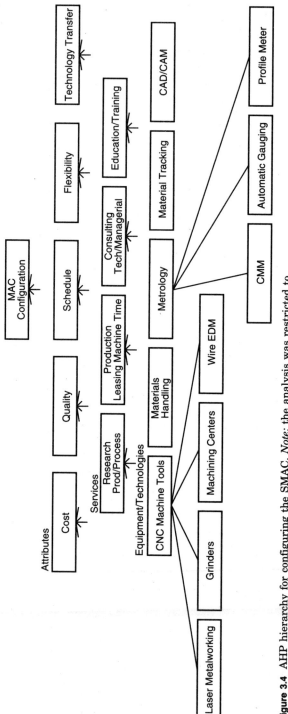

Figure 3.4 AHP hierarchy for configuring the SMAC. *Note:* the analysis was restricted to the first four levels. The additional levels here may be added if deemed necessary.

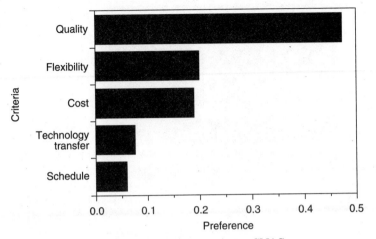

Figure 3.5 Relative preference of criteria for using SMAC.

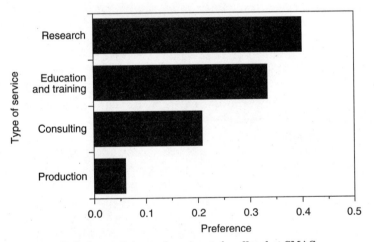

Figure 3.6 Relative preference of services to be offered at SMAC.

The results of the AHP model will provide accurate and consistent customer priorities for the services and the equipment for the SMAC. These priorities can be used as the basis for arriving at the final configuration for the SMAC.

As an example, relative preferences of one of the subjects that participated in configuring and equipping the Pittsburgh SMAC are illustrated in Figs. 3.5, 3.6, and 3.7. These preferences were calculated using a standard AHP software: *EXPERT CHOICE* from Decision Support Software, Inc.

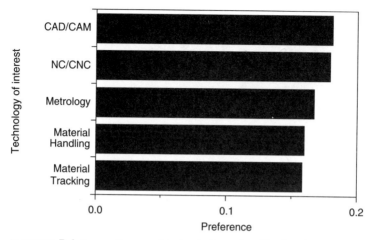

Figure 3.7 Relative preference of technologies to be offered at SMAC.

Figure 3.5 shows preferences of attributes that would result in the most useful SMAC configuration, based on pairwise comparisons of all the attributes in level 2 of the AHP hierarchy. It is apparent from the figure that a SMAC configuration that would improve the user's manufacturing quality is most preferred. Figure 3.6 shows preferences of services to be offered at the SMAC. Assistance in product-process research and education and training emerged as the most preferred services that the SMAC could offer. The technology preferences are shown in Fig. 3.7. Computer-aided design (CAD), computer-aided manufacturing (CAM), and computer numerically controlled (CNC) technologies are high on the list of technologies of interest at the SMAC.

A weighted average of preferences of 10 potential users of the facility along with their probablility of participation in the center were used to guide the initial configuration development. This configuration was further validated through in-depth interviews with potential user organizations to arrive at the final configuration for the Pittsburgh SMAC.

Additional work packages. Additional work packages to be carried during this phase include:

- Design, engineering, construction, and start-up
- Final machine tool and system specification
- Preparation of RFP for design, engineering, and construction of the SMAC
- Review of proposals, negotiation and award of contract(s)

- Procurement and installation of the production equipment
- Staffing and training of the plant managers and professionals
- Procurement of initial special tooling
- Procurement of initial inventory of materials
- Design, testing, and implementation of the management system for the plant
- Initial start-up of the plant
- Development of a strategy for the use of the SMAC to include (1) identification of the initial users, (2) negotiation and consummation of cooperative working agreements with the users, (3) scheduling of the users, (4) design and development of supporting technical data and administrative documentation to support user needs, and (5) pilot testing of the user strategy for the SMAC.

Trial and launch

Previous experiences have indicated that these are long-term and evolutionary projects requiring at least a year of trial involving a "shakedown" of both the plant and the strategy that is being used to operate the plant. System integration and troubleshooting of the plant needs to be done with significant input from the users. In particular, the interfaces with local small and midsized manufacturers will be an important part of the trial and the launch phases. Some of the key work packages involved in these phases of the project include:

- Pilot operation of the SMAC
- Final negotiation and execution of working agreements with local users
- Verification of the SMAC performance
- Evaluation of the efficacy of the SMAC by local manufacturers
- Integration of the technical and management systems

SMAC: Organizational Design

Once the SMAC is established, its successful management depends on a suitable organizational design and a clear definition of authority-responsibility-accountability relationships. A *functional structure* is characterized by extensive policies and procedures, centralized authority, and high specialization. A *project structure* is on the other end of the continuum, with respect to policies and procedures, authority, and specialization. The functional structure emphasizes efficiency and production, while the project structure emphasizes flexibility and adaptability.

A *matrix structure* results from a balanced compromise between a functional structure and a project structure. It is a structure that results from superimposing a project structure on a functional structure. The successful management of SMACs requires efficient management of human and nonhuman resources without compromising flexibility. SMACs will handle a variety of projects involving a number of small organizations with diverse interests. A matrix type of organization structure was considered appropriate for the Pittsburgh SMAC. Project teams with appropriate members from different functional groups will be formed to work on individual customer projects.

Strategic Issues Facing SMACs

A "strategic issue" is a central and essential matter of concern about an organizational strategy having long-term ramifications for the organization or for the project. Identifying the potential strategic issues in a project as soon as possible is important so that each issue can be studied, evaluated, and appropriate strategies developed to eliminate the probable effects of the issue altogether, or at least reduce its potential impact on the performance. During the various stages of the MAC project, several strategic issues became apparent. These issues were:

Awareness of concept. The concept of shared manufacturing is relatively new in the United States. The awareness of its benefits and subsequent acceptance by the manufacturing community are essential if such centers are to succeed.

Customer involvement. A good understanding of the customer needs and customer involvement in the design and configuration of the SMACs can result in better acceptance of the center. In view of this, a detailed manufacturing demographic study and a well-planned needs assessment survey are critical.

Complexity. Two major concerns in the management of SMACs are (1) scheduling and (2) protecting the proprietary interests of the users. These concerns have to be addressed to the satisfaction of the users.

Pricing. The mission of these centers, particularly the ones that receive public funds, is to assist the area manufacturers in improving their global competitiveness. If the pricing is substantially below the market price, we may drive out those businesses we intend to help in the first place. On the other hand, higher prices may threaten the viability of such centers.

Obsolescence. One of the objectives of SMACs is to provide access to modern manufacturing technologies for their users. Given the shorter life cycles and high costs of machine tools, this is a formidable challenge. Shared manufacturing centers should develop strategies for periodic capital equipment replacements. Leasing machine tools instead of buying, upgrading, buy back, and revenue sharing arrangements with machine tool vendors are some of the ways proposed.

Changing market needs. The market needs are dynamic. Procedures should be in place to continuously monitor users' satisfaction and their evolving needs.

References

1. Adams, John R., and Stephen E. Brandt, "Behavioral Implications of the Project Life Cycle," in David I. Cleland and William King (eds.), *Project Management Handbook,* VNR Company, New York, 1983.
2. Cooper, Robert G., "A Process Model for Industrial New Product Development," *IEEE Transactions in Engineering Management,* vol. EM-30, no. 1, February 1983, pp. 2–11.
3. Archibald, Russell D., *Managing High-Technology Programs and Projects,* Wiley, New York, 1976.
4. Bonoma, Thomas V., and Benson P. Shapiro, *Segmenting the Industrial Market,* Lexington Books, Toronto, 1983.
5. Kotler, Philip, *Marketing Management,* 4th ed., Prentice-Hall, Englewood Cliffs, NJ, 1980, pp. 194–213.
6. Bond, C.P., "Targeting a Science Park to Its Task and Market," in J. M. Gibb (ed.), *Science Parks and Innovation Centers: Their Economic and Social Impact,* Elsevier, Amsterdam, 1985, pp. 135–140.
7. Cleland, D. I., B. Bidanda, S. R. Dharwadkar, K. Kahn, and C. Mullins, *U-PARC Flexible Manufacturing Facility,* Final Report for EDA Grant 01-29-03001, Department of Industrial Engineering, University of Pittsburgh, September 1990.
8. Gordon, T.J., and O. Helmer, *Report on a Long Range Forecasting Study,* Paper 2982, Rand Corporation, September 1984.
9. Cleland, David I., and Dundar F. Kocagulu, *Engineering Management,* McGraw-Hill, New York, 1981.
10. Saaty, Thomas L., *Decision Making for Leaders,* Pittsburgh, 1986.
11. Meredith, Jack R., and Nallan C. Suresh, "Justification Techniques for Advanced Manufacturing Technologies," *International Journal for Production Research,* September–October 1986.
12. Sullivan, William G., "Models IEs Can Use to Include Strategic, Non-Monetary Factors in Automation Decisions," *Industrial Engineering,* vol. 18, no. 3, March 1986, pp. 42–50.
13. Khorramshahgol, R., A. Azani, and Yvon Gousty, "An Integrated Approach to Project Evaluation and Selection" (appeared as Technical Management Notes), *IEEE Transactions on Engineering Management,* vol. 35, no. 4, November 1988, pp. 265–270.
14. Wabalickis, Roger N., "Justification of FMS with the Analytical Hierarchy Process," *Journal of Manufacturing Systems,* vol. 7, no. 3, March 1988, pp. 175–182.

4

Developing a Shared Manufacturing Center —A Project Management Approach

To design and develop a manufacturing assistance center is to create something that does not currently exist. In doing this, the use of proven project management processes and techniques is recommended. In this chapter an overview of project management will be given to include a description of the use of project management in conceptualizing and bringing a shared manufacturing assistance center (SMAC) into operation.

Project Management

Formal project management gained impetus with its application to military weapon systems in the early 1950s. Its origins can be traced to the Manhattan Project, the Polaris Submarine program, large construction projects, or the use of naval task forces. Project management is a philosophy and process for the management of ad hoc activities in organizations. A project is a unique, ad hoc group of resources which, when conceptualized, developed, and produced, leads to a *product, service, or organizational process* which has not existed before in the organization, which leads to something in the inventory of resources of the organization that did not previously exist. Developing a new product or a new manufacturing or marketing process, building a manufacturing plant, and building a new highway are examples of the types of projects that can be managed using time-tested and proven project management techniques. A project consists of a combination of organizational resources pulled together to create an added performance capability for a project owner.

Projects are building blocks in the design and execution of organizational strategies and involve four basic considerations:

- What will the project cost?
- What time will be required to bring the project results into being?
- What additional performance capabilities will the project results provide the organization?
- How will the project results fit into the objectives and mission of the enterprise?

A project manager is put in charge of the project. A conceptual model of a project management system (PMS) can best be portrayed by using a *project management systems* approach. In this approach several subsystems are used in managing the project. Figure 4.1 depicts these subsystems. A description of these subsystems follows.

The *facilitative organizational subsystem* is the organizational design of the project. When the project organization is superimposed on the functional organization, a "matrix" organization results. The formal authority and responsibility of the matrix organization provide for the project manager to act as the focal point for the management of the project. Functional managers provide the resources so that the project team members can furnish the technical expertise needed to make the project a reality.

A project is carried out within the *cultural ambience* of the enterprise. Much of the cultural ambience of the organization is related to how the people feel about the way in which the environment of the organization facilitates the accomplishment of organizational ends. The emotional patterns of the social groups, the perceptions of the members of the groups, their attitudes, prejudices, experiences, ethics, morals, and way of thinking about the organization all go into the local cultural ambience of the enterprise.

There are no peopleless organizations—yet all too often we see organizations that fail to facilitate the effective and efficient employment of people in accomplishing organizational objectives and goals. Motivation and the satisfaction of personal and organizational needs come to focus in the people of the organization. Loyalty, trust, commitment, support, and a sense of belonging are all tied together in the sociology, psychology, and communications of the project team. The leadership abilities of the project manager ultimately determine how effective the organization is in using projects as basic building blocks in the design and execution of organizational strategies. It is in the *human subsystem* that all the complexities and vagaries of people come into play. An effective project management system is

Utility Strategic Planning
and Surveillance System

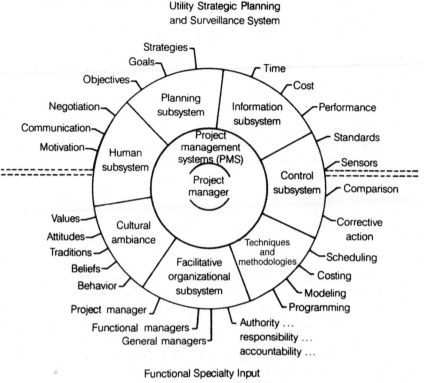

Functional Specialty Input
(Design, Engineering, Procurement, Construction, Quality
Assurance/Quality Control, Licensing, Startup, Operation)

Figure 4.1 The project management system. (Adapted from D. I. Cleland, "Defining a Project Management System," *Project Management Quarterly,* 1977, X, 4, p. 39.)

simply not possible without the effective leadership of people in carrying out the purposes of the project.

To accomplish the project ends, an effective *project planning subsystem* must be designed and implemented. The project plan provides the standards against which control policies, procedures, and mechanisms are measured. Project planning starts with the development of a *work breakdown structure* which shows how the total project is divided up into its basic "work packages." Project schedules and budgets are developed, technical performance goals are selected, and organizational authority and responsibility are established for members of the project team. Project planning also involves identifying the financial and other resources needed to support the project during its life cycle. An important part of project planning is the development of a life cycle model for the project and the identification of work packages that will be developed and implemented during the appropriate life cycle phase of the project.

The management of any organization requires timely and accurate information. The *project management information subsystem* contains the data and the intelligence needed to manage the project—to take the project through its life cycle leading to the creation of a successful product, service, or process for the organization. The basic information required to manage the project includes cost, schedule, technical performance, and intelligence on how the project fits into the overall design and execution of organizational strategies. This subsystem may provide both formal and informal intelligence on how things are going on the project and is obtained from formal project progress reports, from status review meetings, or through conversation with members of the project team. Whatever its source, project information is needed throughout the project during its life cycle.

The *project control subsystem* provides for the selection of performance standards for the project's schedule, budget, and technical performance parameters. This subsystem compares actual progress with planned progress and initiates corrective action as required. In managing the control subsystem, the project team recognizes the need for monitoring the various organizational units that perform work on the project. An effective control system provides the project team and other interested parties with the ongoing status of the project at all times.

Taken as a systems model in the context of a project management philosophy, a project management systems approach helps to ensure that the right things are done on the project, at the right time, leading to the effective and efficient utilization of resources on the project and ultimately producing the desired project results which support organizational purposes.

Project management is carried out through the strategic management framework of the enterprise.

The Strategic Management Framework

Project *planning, organizing, and control* are the major functions carried out in the management of a project. Planning involves thinking through the possibilities and probabilities of the project's future and making an explicit assessment of the need for resources to support the project. The project organization deals with how project resources are aligned, and how authority and responsibility are delineated. Project control is the process of monitoring, evaluating, and comparing planned project results with actual results to determine how the project is doing with respect to its cost, schedule, and technical performance parameters.

Projects are building blocks in the design and execution of organizational strategies. The design and building of a shared manufacturing assistance center is a project activity which when completed provides an added strategic resource for the *strategic management* of the organization by the project owner. When completed, the university will have an additional capability to support its mission of generating and disseminating engineering knowledge, skills, and attitudes. The SMAC will provide a resource for local industry and educational institutions in support of the mission and objectives of these organizations.

Overall organizational planning, sometimes called strategic planning, for both the project and the "bundle of services" that the project will provide, is an important first step in determining the future resource requirements for the project. Organizational planning consists of a rational and rigorous determination of the following planning elements:

- The *mission* is the principal business of the organization. The mission of the Pittsburgh-based SMAC (hereafter called MAC) is "to provide a facility which provides shared manufacturing systems capabilities to include manufacturing technologies, facilities, equipment, and management systems for small and midsized manufacturers in the GPA." The organizational mission is a general and important strategic choice made by the University of Pittsburgh School of Engineering in its role in engineering teaching and research. The implications of this mission are profound: If properly designed and executed, this mission will have a singular and important impact on state-of-the-art capabilities of small and midsized manufacturers in the GPA. An organizational mission is supported by objectives.

- An *objective* is an ongoing end purpose that must be achieved in support of an organizational mission. A computer company defines one of its objectives as "leapfrog the state-of-the-art in hardware technology every five years." A manufacturer defines one of its objectives as "manufacture and deliver the highest of quality in the products provided to our fully satisfied customer." Some of the objectives of the MAC include:

  - "Provide quality manufacturing services to our clients.
  - Provide a laboratory site for manufacturing systems engineering research and development.
  - Provide a facility for small and midsized GPA manufacturers to develop products and associated manufacturing processes."

- Organizational objectives are supported by goals.

■ An organizational *goal* is a milestone in the design and execution of organizational strategies such as a performance goal to improve the quality of products by a certain date. One company stated a goal when it disseminated the statement: "We intend by the end of 1991 to have a flexible manufacturing greenfield facility operational to support corporate strategic plans." A key goal of the MAC is to be operational by mid-1993.

■ An organizational *strategy* is the design of the means through the use of resources to accomplish objectives and goals, thereby contributing to the attainment of the mission of the enterprise. Strategies include action plans, policies, procedures, resource allocation schemes, programs, and—as mentioned earlier—projects.

One of the key strategies for the MAC is that planning will be required to acquire and use the financial resources needed to develop and put the center in an operational mode. Support for the feasibility study of the market need for the GPA came from the U.S. Department of Commerce (Economic Development Administration). Future financial strategies developed for financial support of the center included additional grants from the Economic Development Administration, the U.S. Department of Commerce, Ben Franklin Technology Center of Western Pennsylvania, foundations, and philanthropists. Other potential sources for funding include the U.S. Department of Defense, and local and state agencies. Part of the funding for the MAC after the center is up running will be revenues provided by the users of the center. Substantial start-up and initial operating financial resources will be required in addition to the funds required to design, build, and equip the facility.

The organizational *mission, objectives, goals, and strategies* provide for those resources required to support the MAC project both during its development and in its operation.

Once a preliminary statement of the objective of the project is put forth, action can be taken to develop a project plan. A basic consideration in the development of the project plan is to go through a *work breakdown structure* analysis of the project.

The Work Breakdown Structure (WBS)

The WBS is a product-oriented family tree division of hardware, software, services, and other work elements which organizes, defines, and graphically displays the product, service, or process—in other words, the *results* that the project is intended to produce. A *work package* (WP) is a unit of work required to complete a specific job, such as a piece of hardware, a report, or an element of software, which when taken together with other work packages make up the project in its totality.

In the development of the WBS, a scheme is developed for dividing the project into subelements; major groups are divided into tasks, tasks are subdivided into subtasks, and so on. The organization of a WBS should follow an orderly identification scheme; each WBS element is given a distinct identifier. For example, a WBS for an aircraft would look like this:

1.0 Aircraft

1.1 Fuselage

1.2 Engines

1.3 Wings

1.4 Communications equipment

1.5 Ground support equipment

1.6 And so on

A graphic representation of the WBS and its associated work packages can facilitate its understanding.

The WBS can serve many purposes in the management of a project. These purposes include:

- A pictorial model of all the products, services, and processes that are involved in the project.

- A way to show the interrelationships of the work packages to each other, to the overall project, and to other organizational activities.

- The specific delegation of authority and responsibility to individuals on the project team in the "matrix" context of the organizational elements through which the project is managed.

- A unit of the project for which costs, schedules, and risk assessment can be carried out by the appropriate project team member who is an expert in the matters under consideration.

- Provide a focus through which the application of resources on the project can be monitored, evaluated, and controlled. If corrective action is required, the project work package becomes the center of attention through which corrective action such as replanning, reprogramming, or reallocation can be carried out.

- Gives the project team members a reference point for getting committed to the project.

The WBS provides a common identifier for communicating about the project during its management. The status of the project in terms of its cost, schedule, and technical performance parameters can be best determined by working through the project's work packages. If the status of a particular work package is not known, the status of the overall project is in doubt.

Project Costs

The estimate of the project costs should be done by the experts either on the project team or available through the organizational units that have the wherewithal to do cost analysis and estimating. The development of credible cost estimates is essential in controlling the application of resources on the project. The cost estimates can be used to predict funding requirements for the project. Once the project effort is under way, a comparison of actual with planned costs is essential to keep the project costs under control. Monthly or weekly cost breakdowns for each work package of the project are essential. These cost breakdowns can be integrated into a report available to the project team which shows actual cost with estimated costs with target worker hours and resource allocation.

The project cost estimates are integrated into the appropriate *cost account* in the accounting system of the organization. A cost account usually represents a specific work package identified by the WBS, usually tracked by information on a daily or weekly time report which in turn ties in with the overall organizational cost accounting systems. The cost accounting organization can be expected to provide support to the project team in the estimating and management of the cost parameter of the project.

Project Schedule

The master and work package schedules reflected in a graphic or logic network model are necessary to deal with the time element of the project in which worker and equipment loading can be performed on the project. There are many types of scheduling techniques that can be used, ranging from the basic and simple types like bar charts and milestone charts to the network techniques which use variations of PERT and critical path methodology (CPM). Many software packages are available for both schedule and cost management. Manual techniques are useful for projects that have less than 100 work packages. For larger, more complex projects, software techniques are a must. The references at the end of the chapter can be used if complex scheduling techniques are anticipated.

Bar charts which consist of a scale divided into units of time (days, weeks, months, or even years) across the top of the chart with a listing of the project work packages on the left side of the chart are the most common type. Bars or lines are used to indicate the schedule and status of each work package in relation to the time scale. Bar charts are easy to develop and maintain; they are easy to understand, as they provide a simple picture of the time frame of the project. A variation of the bar chart is the milestone chart, which replaces the bar with lines and triangles to indicate project status. Bar charts are easy to prepare but show limited information on the interrelationships and logic of the work package interdependence.

"Full desk" scheduling techniques can suffice if the number of work packages does not exceed approximately 100. This scheduling technique is done in the following way. Write the work packages on 3 by 5 cards and use the top of a desk or table to put these work packages in the logical relationship and time sequence. Have members of the project team work together around the table to put the cards in their proper place. During the placement of the cards, discussions about the logic and rationale for the placement of the cards can be carried out. After general agreement is reached, a camera can be used to take pictures of the tabletop. After a few days have gone by and people have had time to think about the schedule, get the team together again around the table to verify, or change as needed, the layout of the cards. Take another picture and encourage team members to think about the rationale of the schedule. After this process has been carried out a few times, resulting in a good schedule, the schedule can be put into its permanent form for inclusion in the project plan.

Technical Performance

The technical performance parameter of the project concerns the "bundle of services" that the project results will provide to the project owner. A project to develop a new airliner will provide the airline company with an addition to its inventory of aircraft which provides an added airlift capability. This capability could be measured in passenger and freight capacity of the aircraft, its range, operating altitude, operating efficiency, and its aesthetics. The technical performance parameters of a SMAC project could be the promise of effectiveness in providing a "bundle of services" in the management and technology of manufacturing systems made available to the SMAC users.

Measurement and assessment of the technical performance parameters of a project are difficult. As a shared manufacturing center project is undergoing development, the progress that is being made to satisfy the performance parameters can be determined through the professional judgment of the experts who are on the project team. These team members in turn can call upon the experts who provide backup in the functional elements of the organization. Both the general and the detail specifications of the project can be used to establish benchmarks against which comparison can be made to judge the progress that is being made in reaching the desired performance specifications. As the project is reviewed on a regular basis, discussions should be held concerning what progress is being made vis-à-vis what was desired in the satisfaction of the performance objectives. The technical and management literature on the project can be examined for further benchmarks that can be used in judging how well the project is doing in moving toward the completion.

The Financial Plan

The financial plan involves the development of strategies for obtaining and managing the funds needed to support the project through some sort of organizational authorization process to commit and obligate project monies. The project manager should have residual authority and responsibility for the allocation of the project monies. Most organizations have a document, often titled a *work authorization form,* through which monies can be given to the functional elements of the organization and to outside vendors to use in supporting the project. These work authorization forms usually include the following information: (1) the responsible individual and organization, (2) a work package identification, (3) a schedule, (4) a cost estimate, (5) a funding citation, and (6) a statement of the scope of work to be done. Usually the work authorization form is a one-sheet format; it should be considered as a written contract between the project manager and the persons and organizations supporting the project. The work authorization form, and the information it contains, serve as valuable information in the execution and control of resources on the project.

Supporting Organizational Plans

Each functional organization which supports the project through the designated project team member should have a backup plan which supports the project activities. For example, manufacturing engineering would have a detailed plan on how the project would be supported in manufacturing once the project is committed to production; after-sales service would have detailed plans on how the project's products would be supported after delivery to the customers.

Having an appropriate organizational design for the management of the MAC is an early challenge in the management of the MAC.

The Organizational Design

Planning for the organizational design of a SMAC requires that authority and responsibility be dealt with in a forthright manner as soon as possible in the life cycle of the project. The biggest challenge in organizing for the management of the project centers around how the cross-functional membership of the project team supporting the project will be described and operated.

One of the more important parts of project planning is to develop an explicit plan on how the authority and responsibility will be allocated among the project team members. The biggest challenge in getting the project team organized is to describe—and have this description accepted—the team members' relationship to the project manager and to their supervisors in the functional unit of the organizations supporting the project. When a project team is organized across the functional elements of the organization, a "matrix" organizational design is created. In the matrix configuration the project team members report to *both* the project manager and their functional supervisors. A model of the matrix organization is shown in Fig. 4.2.

In this matrix organization a violation of the management principle of "unity of command" is suspected. Such a violation can exist if care is not taken to describe the relative authority and responsibility of the team members vis-à-vis the project manager and the functional supervisors. The key to an understanding and acceptance of the matrix organization centers around the work package that is found at the interface of the project and functional effort in the organization. In Fig. 4.2, this interface is depicted with a large X and titled in the lower right-hand corner of the matrix organization as portrayed. The running lines in the figure portray the horizontal effort of the project. The functional effort in Fig. 4.2 is portrayed in the traditional organizational chart form—usually a solid line indicating the formal flow of authority and responsibility.

Clarity of the matrix organization is enhanced *if* the syntax of the statements describing the relative authority and responsibility is developed, understood, and accepted by the members of the project team and the key personnel in the functional elements supporting the project. Table 4.1 shows these statements, which should be reflected in policy documents of the organization, thereby enhancing their acceptance as a guide to the way people should think about their role in the interdependent and complementary matrix organization.

In the matrix organization the team member relates vertically to the functional organization, and horizontally to the project team. However, on any project there are usually many other people and organizations that have, or believe that they have, a vested interest or claim against the project. Often called *project stakeholders,* these

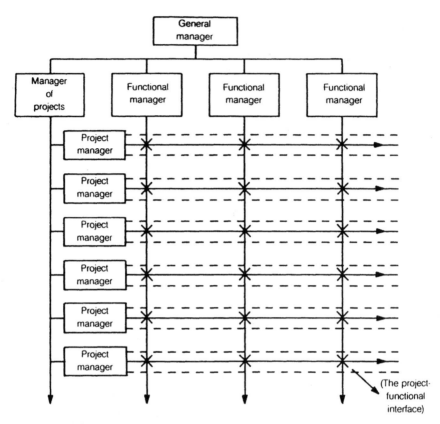

Figure 4.2 A basic project management matrix. (Source: D. I. Cleland, *Project Management: Strategic Design and Implementation,* Tab Professional and Reference Books, Blue Ridge Summit, Pa., p. 137.)

TABLE 4.1 The Project-Functional Interface

Project manager	Functional manager
What is to be done?	How will the task be done?
When will the task be done?	Where will the task be done?
Why will the task be done?	Who will do the task?
How much money is available to do the task?	How well has the functional input been integrated into the project?
How well has the total project been done?	

Source: D.I. Cleland, *Project Management: Strategic Design and Implementation*, TAB Professional and Reference Books, Blue Ridge Summit, Pa., 1990, p. 142.

stakeholders can be supportive or destructive of the project and its ultimate outcome.

Stakeholder Claims

In the development of any project there are vested interests that wish to share in the benefits of the project results. There may also be vested interests that see the project as threatening the existing order, introducing a change that is not wanted, or reducing the perceived well-being of a group of constituents. Political, economic, social, legal, technological, competitive, and even emotional purposes will, to some degree, impact any project. For example, a decision to design, build, and operate an "automated factory" is a key strategic decision for a manufacturing company. On the surface such a decision, which would likely result in more manufacturing flexibility leading to lower product cost, higher quality, and better competition, seems logical and immune to the resistance of anyone involved. But who is involved? The answer—anyone or any organization that sees something to be gained or lost by the automated factory. These stakeholders could include:

- Project team members who are concerned with the management and delivery of the automated factory project results on time and within budget.

- General and senior members of the organization who are responsible for the integration of the automated factory into the strategic management of the enterprise.

- The manufacturing manager and staff who are responsible for making the new automated factory work in an efficient and effective manner.

- Vendors who see the opportunity to sell products and services.

- Local union(s) who see important changes coming that will change the quality and quantity of the work force, which will likely have an impact on union membership and future relations with the plant manager and staff.

- Employees who see the automated factory reducing the number of workers and the need for the remaining ones to learn new knowledge, skills, and attitudes.

- Community leaders who see the automated plant having both desirable and unwanted changes in the local community.

- Customers having an expectation of lower-cost, higher-quality products being delivered on a more timely basis than was done under traditional manufacturing.

- Local, state, and federal governments who have ordinances and laws governing the operation of the automated factory.

- Politicians who will be concerned about the influence of the automated factory on the political game that they play. For example, the new automated factory, with its promise of greater efficiencies and effectiveness, may result in the closing of some traditional factories in both the local area and elsewhere in the country.

The list goes on and on; each project will have both its generic and unique set of stakeholders to be considered and dealt with in the management of the project. The management of the stakeholders is essential for ensuring success of the project and should be approached through the development of a formal stakeholder management process. The details of such a formal process are beyond the purview of this book. The reader is encouraged to review Ref. 1.

In the management of a project, the project team has to determine how these vested interests or stakeholders are likely to react to the project decisions, what influence their reaction will carry, and how the stakeholders might interact with each other and with influential political, social, economic, legal, and competitive leaders in aiding or "shooting the project through the eyes," thereby preserving or extending the stakeholders' interests.

A Project Plan Summary

A project plan is like a map—it can guide the project team on the general route to be undertaken in starting, continuing, and finishing a project. Plans are a detail of the specifications and simulation of the future of the project. Project planning should result in a "living document" to be kept current as the project progresses. The major work packages to be undertaken in the development of a project plan include those activities likely to produce a realistic plan. In the context of a manufacturing assistance center the following work packages can be undertaken in the design, development, and start-up of the center:

- *Establish the strategic linkage of the center.* The Pittsburgh MAC is a building block in the design and execution of strategies to provide assistance in manufacturing systems for designated regional small and midsized manufacturers. When operational, the MAC will provide a resource center for the improvement of users' manufacturing systems capability.

- *Develop the technical performance objective of the proposed MAC.* The MAC objective is to provide a state-of-the-art manufacturing systems facility for the sharing of manufacturing systems knowledge, skills, and attitudes for research, development, education, and training for small to medium-sized firms located in the region. The configuration of the Pittsburgh MAC will consist of a set of computerized numerical control machining tools for machining operations, laser metalworking machine tools, automated material handling equipment, and robots. Computer-aided design workstations with solid modeling software will give the MAC a strong product-design capability. Material tracking will consist of the state-of-the-art automatic identification equipment.

- *Describe the project through the development of the project WBS.* Develop a product-oriented family tree division of the hardware, software, services, and other tasks to organize, define, and display the MAC as well as the work to be accomplished to achieve the specific configuration and modus operandi of the MAC. The development of the MAC was described earlier in this chapter.

- *Identify and make provisions for the assignment of the functional work packages.* In the case of the MAC this involved gaining the cooperation of different specialists in the University of Pittsburgh. This included those specialists in research proposal preparation, cost and schedule estimating, contract negotiation and administration, industrial engineering, manufacturing engineering, and manufacturing management, and assistance from the government relations department of the university.

- *Identify the work packages that will be subcontracted.* In the MAC proposal this includes provisions for an independent architectural and engineering (A&E) evaluation of the building donated by the university for the center. An A&E firm will be employed to do the A&E work for the modification of the building, to supervise the construction work, and to work with the team that will install the manufacturing equipment. Machine tool manufacturers, software development firms, and production planning organizations will be engaged to provide professional services for the development and start-up of the manufacturing center.

- *Develop the master and work packages.* A master schedule will be prepared based on the work packages developed during the early part of the project planning phase. This schedule will include the logic networks and relationships of the project work packages as well as the time dimensions of the schedule. This schedule will be coordinated with the Industrial Engineering Department chairperson and with the Dean of the School of Engineering to ensure compatibility with other commitments of the school.

- *Identify the "strategic issues" likely to impact the MAC.* A strategic issue is a condition or pressure, either internal or external, that will have a significant effect on one or more factors of the project, such as its financing, design, engineering, construction, and operation.* Some of the more relevant strategic issues facing the MAC project include the willingness of small and midsized manufacturers to participate in the center and the availability of monies for the design, construction, and start-up of the center. In addition, the availability of start-up and operational funds to support these centers until they become self-supporting is a critical issue that must be considered.

- *Estimate project costs.* Determine what will be the likely costs of the project, including an assessment of the probability of staying within the estimated costs. These costs were estimated for (1) capital equipment and facility costs, (2) center operating costs, and (3) project continuation costs. Project continuation costs represent the cost of updating and refining the concept of the center. The center director and supporting costs were the core of the project continuation costs. Center operating costs include the direct costs of personnel needed to staff the MAC. Capital equipment costs represent the cost of the building and machine and computer tools needed to operate the MAC to assist local manufacturers.

- *Perform risk analysis.* Establish the probability and degree of a setback in the development, start-up, and operation of the MAC. The greatest risk was considered to be the lack of participation by stakeholders in the project. While it is conceded that not all participants and sponsors would be fully satisfied, it is imperative that efforts be made early in the project, and continued as needed, to identify and deal with the many factors that could contribute to nonparticipation by stakeholders. In the feasibility study it was determined that a major obstacle for the center could be the public misconception about its mission. That is, users might perceive the center as a competitor and would elect not to participate. Another risk was the possibility that users would fear the loss of proprietary information which could jeopardize their competitive position. These concerns and risk factors suggest that the center strategy must be implemented to ensure confidentiality and exclusivity of user products and services. In addition, the center should be

---

*Definition derived from chaps. 1, 4, and 15 of Ref. 2. This reference also provides guidance on how to direct strategic issues in the management of organizational affairs.

managed so that responsiveness to users' needs, concerns, and interests can be done clearly in a profile of confidentiality and with an avowed purpose of service provided on a not-for-profit basis.

- *Develop the project budgets, funding plans, and other resource plans.* Establish how the project budget should be managed and how the funds should be utilized, and what information is needed to ensure that an expeditious and careful funding of resources to support the center is carried out. This should include the development of an interface with university financial and accounting offices so that adequate information and strategies are in place to deal with the financial aspects of the center in a forthright, ethical, and legal manner.

- *Select the organizational design.* The design of the organizational structure of the matrix and its associated work packages comprises the major consideration in getting the project organized. The major theoretical elements of organizing a project are presented elsewhere in this chapter. The development of policies, procedures, information needs and uses, the development of the project team, the assessment and strengthening of the culture for the project, and how the project administration will be carried out are also included in this work package.

In the organizational design for the Pittsburgh MAC, three domains of spheres of influence were taken into consideration. Figure 4.3 shows the organizational design of these three domains:

Strategic management domain. This domain involves the design and implementation of actions leading to the designation of the MAC mission, objectives, goals, and strategies. MAC research projects will be submitted through this domain and will undergo review and funding by the appropriate agencies. Surveillance of funded research projects will be maintained by the existing administrative structure of the University of Pittsburgh, School of Engineering. The executive management of the MAC will be carried out by the codirectors within the Industrial Engineering Department reporting to the dean of the School of Engineering. These directors will have residual responsibility for the results produced by the MAC and will have delegated authority for its effective and efficient operation, making sure there is an appropriate interface with the GPA user community.

Research project domain. This domain is the sphere of influence within the center where research projects will be conceptualized, prepared, and executed. This domain will parallel the academic departments and programs of the university. Both departmental

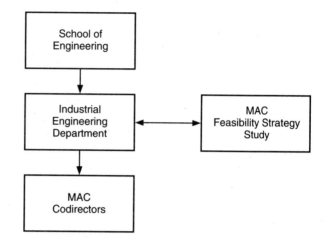

Strategic Management Domain:

• Design and Implementation of MAC Mission, Objectives, Goals, and Strategies

• Research Project Proposal Review, Funding Assistance, and Surveillance

• MAC Greater Pittsburgh "Stakeholder" Interface Management

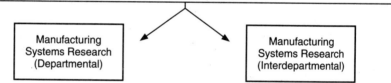

Research Project Domain:

• Research Project Conceptualization and Design

• Research Proposal Preparation

• Individual and Team Faculty Research to Advance Professionalism

• Research Project Development and Execution

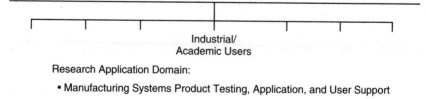

Research Application Domain:

• Manufacturing Systems Product Testing, Application, and User Support

• Technical Documentation

• Education and Training

Figure 4.3 A sample organizational design—MAC project.

and interdepartmental manufacturing systems research will be carried out in this domain. Special efforts will be made to encourage, protect, and facilitate individual and team faculty research interests in pursuit of professional advancement in this domain.

Research application domain. This domain will provide the focus where the results of research will be carried out in terms of manufacturing systems process testing, application, and user support as needed and indicated in the market survey. The development of technical documentation for use in the context of manufacturing systems engineering to support education, training, product and process improvement, and prototyping and sundry applications will be carried out in this domain. Several organizational units exist which will interact with the MAC.

An important part of the management system for the MAC will be a *board of advisors* to maintain surveillance over the efficiency and effectiveness with which the strategy for the center is designed and executed. The composition of the board of advisors and the selection of the appropriate membership will be undertaken during the next phase in the design and development of the MAC. During this phase the specific responsibilities of the board of advisors will be developed through interaction with the principal users of the MAC.[3] As noted above, the executive management of the MAC will be carried out by the codirectors in the Industrial Engineering Department of the University of Pittsburgh. The research project domain and the research application domain will exercise the authority necessary to discharge their responsibilities to their parent organizations.

- *Develop project control concepts, processes, and techniques.* This work package plan considers how the project's status will be judged through a formal and informal review process. On what basis? How often? By whom? Asking these types of questions can help facilitate the development of a project control philosophy for the project.

A basis must be provided for the *standards* used in carrying out the project management function of control. Project plans and control systems are interdependent forces in the management of a project.

- *Project control.* Control is the process of monitoring, evaluating, and comparing planned results with actual results to determine the status of the project cost, schedule, and technical performance parameters. Effective control requires suitable information that provides insight into how the project is going. The managerial concept of control is often portrayed as depicted in Fig. 4.4. On the MAC project the following elements in the project control cycle were used:

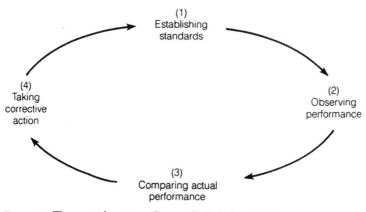

Figure 4.4 The control system. (Source: D. I. Cleland, *Project Management: Strategic Design and Implementation,* Tab Professional and Reference Books, Blue Ridge Summit, PA, p. 212.)

Project standards. A standard is a touchstone. The plan for the development of the MAC provided the basis for developing the technical performance, cost, and schedule standards.

Performance feedback. Feedback comes about through a watchful surveillance of what is happening on the project. On the MAC written reports, letters, memoranda, and other documentation provided insightful feedback. However, the best insight came from the weekly project review meetings where information that was gathered gave insight into how well the project was going.

Comparing planned and actual performance. By comparing the actual with the planned project activities, insight is gained into the questions: How is the project doing? What deviations are appearing, if any? These and similar questions can give insight into what corrective action needs to be taken to get the project back on its track.

Corrective action. This is the development and implementation of strategies to bring about replanning, reprogramming, reallocation, or realignment of resources on the project directed to getting the project back on track. The essence of corrective action is the development of remedial actions to improve the project's performance. On the MAC project almost every weekly meeting provided opportunities where remedial action could be taken by way of emphasizing certain actions—reallocating labor usage, development of new ways of doing things, and in general modifying the project plan in some way to better serve the project's ends.

Corrective action is very much of a people-based activity. People control projects, not computers or information systems or progress reports. Although computer and information technology can provide powerful tools for the generation and comparison of information relative to the project, corrective action has to be taken through the members of the project team.

An important part of the management of a project is the application of life cycle concepts and processes.

One way of describing the life cycle of a manufacturing project is suggested by Hayes et al.[4] The authors make the important point of the importance of senior executives' roles in the project early in the life cycle of the project. According to the authors, the ability of senior management to influence the outcome of a project declines rapidly as it moves from one phase to another in its life cycle. Typically, top managers pay the least attention to the early phases and tend to get involved when a development project approaches market or process implementation. Yet the ability to influence the project in later phases of its life cycle is limited. True, the project can be canceled, but at a considerable cost later in its life cycle. It is better to have senior management maintain surveillance in the early phases when the compatibility of the project results with the evolving strategy of the enterprise can be assessed on an ongoing basis. If the project's technical, market, and competitive realities have been considered early in its life cycle, and a foundation for continuing the project has been determined to exist, then giving clearance for continuing funding can be provided. If not, the project can be canceled and the funds saved can be used for alternative product-process projects.[4]

There are many different ways of describing the life cycle of a project. Each industry tends to have its own parochial way of defining the phases that products and projects go through. This is to be expected because of the diversity and provincial nature of projects.

The life cycle phases in the new product development process as suggested by Cooper were used in Chap. 3 to show how a shared center can be implemented within such a framework.[5]

Summary

In this chapter a general overview of project management has been given. Where possible this overview has shown the application of proven project management processes and techniques to the MAC. Planning, organizing, and control of project activities are major responsibilities of the project team under the leadership of the project manager.

The references at the end of this chapter provide details of project management. Some of the techniques shown are sophisticated—but the sophistication of the techniques used should not exceed the sophistication of the project. A firm philosophy of the role that project management can play in the development, construction, and operation of a SMAC can be most useful. However, a good common sense of what to use in managing the project can pay handsomely.

Projects, like organizations, are in motion as each proceeds along its life cycle. Projects go through a life cycle to completion, hopefully on time, within budget, and satisfying the technical performance objectives of the project. In Chap. 3 we applied the life cycle concept to the development of a shared manufacturing center as part of the project management philosophy we recommend.

We have advanced an approach that can help small and medium-sized manufacturers regain their competitiveness by forming strategic alliances in the form of community-sponsored manufacturing assistance centers. Further, the planning and implementation of these centers follows a methodology similar to the new product development process.

In our exploratory study, several strategic issues became apparent during the conceptualization of the project. These issues were: (1) the acceptability of such a shared manufacturing facility in the community by potential users; (2) the willingness of the small manufacturers to enter into a strategic alliance for the use of the plant and to share proportionately the costs of operating the facility; (3) the availability of equipment from government and other sources; (4) adequate funding support from the state in the design, building, and start-up of the center; (5) the effective use of the plant by university faculty; and (6) maintaining the confidentiality of the work being done by the individual users of the center so as to protect proprietary information.

References

The authors have drawn from Ref. 1 in preparing this chapter.

1. Cleland, David I., *Project Management: Strategic Design and Implementation,* Tab Professional and Reference Books, Blue Ridge Summit, Pa., 1990, chap. 6.
2. King, W. R., and D. I. Cleland (eds.), *Strategic Planning and Management Handbook,* Van Nostrand Reinhold, New York, 1987.
3. Cleland, D. I., B. Bidanda, S. R. Dharwadkar, K. Kahn, and C. A. Mullins, *U-PARC Flexible Manufacturing Facility,* Final Report, University of Pittsburgh Department of Industrial Engineering, Pittsburgh, Pa., September 1990, pp. 54–57.
4. Hayes, Robert H., Steven C. Wheelwright, and Kim B. Clark, *Dynamic Manufacturing—Creating the Learning Organization,* The Free Press, 1988, pp. 278–280.
5. Cooper, Robert G., "A Process Model for Industrial New Product Development," *IEEE Transactions in Engineering Management,* vol. EM-30, no. 1, February 1983, pp. 2–11.

5

Economics, Management Policies, and Accounting Practices for a Shared Flexible Computer Integrated Manufacturing Facility

Ted Lettes and Tip Parker

U.S. Department of Commerce
Washington, D.C.

Introduction

The key elements of competitiveness for manufacturing companies in many of today's global markets are quality, life cycle cost, just-in-time delivery, and the ability to change product rapidly. Flexible computer integrated manufacturing (FCIM) provides a capability to meet these criteria if effectively applied in the context of a company's total business operation.

However, start-up costs are very high and current accounting practices do not consider some important aspects of managing a company

---

Note: This chapter is based in significant part on a paper prepared as part of the authors' official duties as government employees and therefore may not be copyrighted in the United States. The authors choose to use the term "flexible computer integrated manufacturing facility" in lieu of the title used for the book, Shared Manufacturing. This paper is to help businesses, associations, universities, and government agencies develop and evaluate proposals for shared FCIM facilities.

The authors are with the Technology Administration, U.S. Department of Commerce, Washington, D.C. 20230.

with FCIM. Nor do they recognize the new elements of competitiveness which are considered unquantifiable intangibles.

Thus justification of investment in advanced manufacturing is often a leap of faith that is later validated or found to be a mistake. These management limitations provide a major barrier to FCIM adoption, especially for small firms which have to rely on conventional financing sources.

Many recent papers describe the advantages of FCIM systems and how they can change the basic nature of companies that adopt them. There are also writings on how management accounting systems have failed to keep pace with advanced manufacturing technology. But little if anything has been written on the unique options and benefits that several companies can enjoy by sharing an FCIM facility as means for overcoming the accounting, justification, financing, and management growth barriers to modernization.

Because of the multiple interests involved, the success of a shared FCIM facility will depend heavily on the policies it establishes and the management, financial, and accounting practices it adopts.

This paper explains how a shared facility can serve several firms and provide advantages that they cannot obtain independently. The paper is not a research or academic treatise designed to present new knowledge. Instead, it concentrates on practical, managerial issues and suggests alternatives that can be considered.

There are many possible combinations of these alternatives that might be appropriate for particular situations, and in fact, each of the early shared FCIM facilities is based on different choices. The paper indicates how various choices may be interdependent, but it avoids recommendations, as there are no best or right solutions. The most effective alternative depends on the particular circumstances.

Synopsis

This chapter is in three parts. Part 1 presents the foundation on which the analysis is based in three sections:

Assumptions and conventions—sets the limits of the discussion

The economics of flexible computer integrated manufacturing systems—discusses the general economic characteristics of FCIM

Overview of the economics of FCIM sharing—explains the unique aspects of sharing this class of technology

Part 2 presents options for establishing the facility in three sections:

The purpose of the facility—outlines the possible objectives

Analysis of ownership options—examines alternatives for who can own what

Some examples—shows some consequences of combining the factors and choices presented in Parts 1 and 2.

Part 3 explores issues of recording FCIM costs and allocating them to specific products in two sections:

The problem—an explanation with examples

Some possible accommodations—suggestions for shared FCIM facilities and companies that use them

Part 1: The Foundations of This Analysis

Assumptions and conventions

Two sets of assumptions and conventions underlie this analysis.

The Facility and Users.   The assumed FCIM facility consists of a physical site, equipment, software, management, and staff. Its primary purpose is to provide time on advanced manufacturing equipment for a group of client firms. These firms are its customers and the market for its services. They may use the time to learn how to operate and evaluate types of equipment which they might obtain for their own plants, adapt their products to this type of manufacture, train their employees, develop new products, or use shared time to manufacture products on a continuing basis. The client firms may remain as a stable group, or there may be a continuous flow of companies joining and leaving the group.

By assuming the facility is a free-standing entity, we can discuss the manufacturing technology and economic factors of the facility separately from the product and marketing strategies of the client firms. In practice, the facility may be an independent for-profit company, a subsidiary of another firm or nonprofit organization, jointly owned by its client firms, or owned and operated by one of the firms.

The facility can be used to provide education for managers in how to run a company that uses modern manufacturing, and some facilities are being called microteaching factories. We distinguish training (how to perform a known or predictable activity) from education (how to approach a new situation), and the facility can be used to provide both. The facility may also be used for research and education of students by academic institutions.

Characteristics of the Cell.   More for simplicity of discussion than technical accuracy, the facility is assumed to start with a single metalworking cell of multiple machines that can cut, turn, drill, bore, thread, mill, grind, and inspect parts worked from bar stock, castings, or semiforming preprocesses. The machines may be connected by a material handling robot, and the cell is operated under the control of a computer. The cell has sensors which the computer can use to monitor and adjust or halt processes if they vary from specified limits. The cell may use special tools, jigs, and fixtures to form individual parts.

The cell uses existing, off-the-shelf equipment and will probably be modified or upgraded over time. The facility also has a computer-assisted design (CAD) hardware and software system that client firms may use to develop the software or numerical control (NC) data needed to drive the cell.

The key performance features of the cell and CAD system are that within the range of work it is designed to do, it can:

- Consistently produce a type of part at a predictable rate, to specified tolerances, with little or no human attention to product quality or maintenance of process tolerances.

- Concentrate on profitable, small-batch production, looking toward an economic batch size of "one."

- Complete all steps in converting material to finished parts in a continuous sequence without delays, interim storage, or movement of semicompleted parts outside the cell. (Nonmachining operations like heat treating are ignored.)

- Readily shift from making one type of part to another type with minimal setup or idle time.

- Continuously expand its repertoire by "remembering" how to make every type of part it has ever made.

- Pyramid the repertoire by using what it remembers about making one type of part as a basis for making similar but different types, with only the differences being programmed.

A shared facility could be established with much less equipment—a single CAD system or NC machine may be adequate to serve some companies. The assumed cell was selected to illustrate points that will be made later.

The economics of flexible manufacturing systems

There are two striking economic characteristics of a factory that makes extensive use of current FCIM technology.

1. *Start-up costs.*   The first characteristic is the large start-up costs in relation to modest operating costs. This characteristic applies

to the initial facility, each enhancement, and each new product to be made. As a result, determining the manufactured cost of an individual part involves allocating one-time costs and overhead far more than measuring direct costs. Put another way, the costs of producing a particular batch of parts in an FCIM facility are driven or caused by actions taken independently of, and frequently long before, the decision to produce the batch.

In addition to the anticipated start-up costs, there may also be events that produce unplanned or accidental start-up costs. These events typically occur when the various components of hardware and software obtained from different sources are brought together to work as a single system but fail to work as intended. These events may produce cost overruns or less obvious but equally serious shortfalls from planned capabilities where too much is paid for what is obtained.

2. *Computers and Retained Knowledge.* The second characteristic stems from the ability of a facility to learn how to perform a series of operations. Because the facility can remember and build a repertoire of all that it has done, the cost to make a repeat batch of parts can be far less than the cost of the first batch. Similarly, developing a new part as an adaptation of a previously produced part may cost much less than starting from scratch. The more the facility knows how to produce, the lower the cost of adding to its repertoire.

Most of the repertoire is in computer software and NC data that can be kept in confidence, duplicated, shared, or sold. Taking advantage of this characteristic, however, requires familiarity with computers and the ways one must think to use them well.

Each of the following five primary elements of cost of a shared FCIM facility is driven or caused by specific decisions, most of which are made long before any routine production runs:

1. *Capital Equipment.* Except for the building, the facility's largest investment is probably in the machinery comprising the original cell unless this machinery is leased, donated, or obtained at discount prices. The CAD system hardware is a relatively minor investment even though additional CAD equipment may be needed if many firms want to use it.

 The equipment will be depreciated on the basis of anticipated useful life, residual value, number of shifts of use, and expected use rate per shift. It is easy to show how legitimate but different choices among these factors could lead to a range of hourly charges from x dollars to $10x$ dollars for a particular machine.

 Selecting these factors are among the most critical decisions to be made in justifying and measuring the facility. If, for example, the equipment is depreciated on the basis of a one-shift operation, the depreciation charged to its products will be three times greater than if a three-shift operation is planned. But if machine time is priced on the basis of three shifts and that level is not reached, the facility will appear to run at a loss which might have been avoided had a lower use factor been anticipated.

2. *System Software.*   The computer software necessary to link the cell machines with the control computer and link the control computer to the CAD computer is often a mix of purchased software products and individually tailored programs. This software must be operational before the facility begins production, and if it is developed entirely on site, its cost could approach the cost of the equipment.

   Normal accounting practice and tax laws call for this software cost to be treated as an expense when it is developed even though it is for use in future periods. Selecting, developing, and controlling the one-time cost of system software is second only to hardware management for controlling the eventual costs of FCIM products.

3. *Product Technology.*   Once the equipment and system software are operational, the cell must be programmed or "taught" how to make each type of part. Special hardware may be needed and one or more pilot runs may be necessary to test and improve the process. In this analysis, we are calling the combination of steps needed to make a new part or family of parts "product technology."

   Each decision to create new product technology is a cost driver. We would include the setup for the initial or test batch as part of the cost of new product technology, as opposed to the costs of routine setups for subsequent batch runs which we consider to be operating costs. The cost of creating product technology includes the following three items:

   a. *Software and NC Data.*   There are several ways to instruct the cell, ranging from developing the design of a part through the CAD process to putting a robot in a learn mode and manually guiding it through its paces while it creates its own code to repeat what it is being taught. In general, the more this form of programming can build on programs, codes, and data already in the system, the lower the cost for a new type of part.

   b. *Special Tools, Jigs, and Fixtures.*   The efficiency of a repetitive process can often be increased by using hardware such as special cutting tools or devices to hold the work. Decisions to make and use this hardware are usually a function of inventiveness, cost of the hardware, and anticipated savings. With FCIM systems, there may be tradeoffs between what to do with special hardware or with software.

c. *Testing and Debugging.* While computers bring new economies and predictability, they also bring new opportunities to make mistakes. Each time product technology is developed for a new type of parts, it may have to be tested and perhaps modified before it can be used for production.

4. *Operations.* By some estimates, upwards of 90 percent of the cost of making a part with FCIM may be committed before production starts. While there is little of the direct labor that characterized earlier manufacturing, a factory does cost something to run. Here are examples of costs which can be measured and may, to varying degrees, be attributed directly to the product:

   a. *Routine Batch Setup.* While traditional manufacturing attempts to use long production runs to minimize setup costs, one of the advantages of FCIM is low setup cost for economical production of short runs. (An FCIM cell may be less efficient for long runs than more specialized equipment designed for sustained performance of a few operations.) It may be possible to schedule the cell to make sequential batches of similar parts so that little time is spent shifting from one batch to another, but some machine time and labor will probably be needed for most setups. These times and costs are measurable and may be attributed directly to specific batches, particularly if they include adding or removing special hardware. Once the product technology to make a part is fixed, there are two cost drivers for each batch setup. The first is the decision to order the batch, and the second is when it is scheduled in relation to other jobs. Other things being equal, schedule-driven costs may be saved if orders provide enough lead time to optimize setup activities.

   b. *Production.* The direct costs of production are relatively easy to measure. Material, abrasives, lubricants, and tools may be consumed directly. If the cell is attended, there can be direct labor. Electricity can be metered, though judgment may go into setting the rate to charge. These costs are driven more by the quantity, type, and production processes for the parts than by the number of batches.

   c. *Maintenance.* Maintenance costs can be driven by the passage of time, operating hours, types of operation, abuse, and unanticipated failures. Examples of these are:

      (1) *Routine.* Lubrication, checking and adjusting for wear, and reviewing computer-driven self-diagnostic tests are normal maintenance procedures that are intended to prevent costly equipment failure. They can be measured easi-

ly, but judgment may be needed in allocating them to individual production runs.

(2) *Tool Wear and Replacement.* Cutting tools need to be sharpened or replaced, and if desired, computer records can trace their use to individual production batches. But decisions on what types of tools to use and how fast to feed them can be important. Both the volume of production and the choice of process can be tool cost drivers.

(3) *Specific Use Factors.* Some products may require more of a machine's capabilities or cause more rapid deterioration than others. A worn machine may be able to hold to wide tolerances but not meet more demanding requirements. It appears that Japanese firms run machines below their capacity to limit wear. Thus, the type of use may drive some maintenance costs, while actions to avoid wear can lead to increased production time.

(4) *Unusual Events.* Sooner or later, most machines break down or need unscheduled maintenance. Although normally hard to predict, these events may be caused by abuse or the way the machine is used.

5. *Education and Training.* By training, we mean teaching people how to perform the predictable steps of operating the equipment and software to make products. By education, we mean helping managers as well as technical people expand their abilities to think. Put another way, we use training to mean helping people learn how to do tasks that can be anticipated, and education to mean helping people become ready to do things for which they cannot be trained. Running a company that uses FCIM successfully requires new ways of thinking. Both education and training can involve initial and continuing costs, all of which are intended to improve future performance and are hard to link to specific products.

6. *Other Factory Overhead.* Most of the operating costs of the facility will be overhead. These include space charges, heat, light, fire protection, insurance, materials handling outside the cell, purchasing, financial operations, management, and most important—the cost of money. It is necessary to understand the significance and causes of those costs, but they will normally not be driven by decisions to use the cell itself.

The economics of FCIM sharing

Thousands of small and intermediate-size firms that need FCIM systems cannot afford the capital investment, start-up expense, and learning costs necessary to create them. Luckily, FCIM technology is particularly suited to shared development and early use by multiple firms for four basic reasons:

1. Many of the start-up expenses are to produce knowledge which each firm can obtain with others at a fraction of the total cost.
2. Multiple firms can pay their share of the costs of operating the joint facility as they convert their businesses to FCIM operations instead of each having to pay the full cost of obtaining and slowly developing uses for equipment of their own.
3. The shared equipment can be loaded to operating capacity more quickly by a number of client firms, allowing additional capacity to be added in increments that spread the investment over time and phase it to productive use.
4. Large companies may find it easier to work through a shared facility with small firms converting to advanced manufacturing than with each firm individually. The large companies may be interested in the small firms as components sources or as customers if the large firms are sellers of equipment, materials, or services used by the small firms.

An oversimplified way to make this point is that 20 companies can start to use a single cell, load it to capacity, obtain a second cell, load it, and so on until 20 cells are fully loaded, at a much lower total cost than if each company obtains its own cell and gradually brings it up to a full load. Halfway through the cycle, there are 10 fully loaded shared cells and one partially loaded one, in contrast to 20 half-loaded cells if each company obtains its own. The cumulative cash flow curves of these two models are radically different.

The general belief that companies operate independently and will not cooperate was never completely correct, and is changing. Major competitors routinely cross-license patents, small newspapers use joint printing facilities, many firms participate in establishing industry standards, and following recent legislation, there is a growing trend toward cooperative research. Competing companies use common suppliers as multiple airlines use a single food service contractor at an airport and banks use computer service bureaus to process encoded checks. These examples are comparable to some of the ways that FCIM technology can be shared. The economics of sharing fall into five broad categories:

1. *Sharing Research and Training.* Extensive use of FCIM changes almost everything in a company, not just manufacturing. Company strategy, marketing methods, design techniques, make-up of the work force, and accounting systems are prime candidates for change. Throughout a company, people may be shifted back to

the toe of the learning curve and made to reconsider the fundamentals of their jobs.

Much of this cost can be shared among the client firms of either a jointly owned or third-party-owned shared facility. The product engineers of several firms can work together to prepare for automated manufacture by creating system software modules and teaching each other to use them at a fraction of the time and cost of doing it individually. Similarly, the accountants, manufacturing engineers, and market forecasters of several firms can help each other move up their learning curves. The cost of impressive demonstrations to attract prospective customers and sources of operating capital can be shared.

Some client firms may want to monitor or advance the state of the art, and the facility can be the test bed for new equipment, software, and ideas that can be shared on a continuing basis. Finally, equipment and software suppliers may be able to provide more support to a shared facility than they could afford to do for individual small companies.

2. *Sharing Capital Equipment.* The FCIM can be enhanced over time, but a major initial investment (or commitment if leased) is needed to create the nucleus. If a firm were to establish its own cell, it could not begin to recover this investment until it had converted enough of its processes to achieve a satisfactory load factor. With several firms sharing a facility, an economic load factor can be reached more quickly. Equipment suppliers may give discounts to encourage future orders from the facility or client firms. If so, the facility may add additional capacity or a client firm might replicate the cell in its own factory with equipment that it understands at a lower cost than by creating its own cell originally. Options for handling the capital investment are discussed below.

3. *Sharing System Software.* Since computer software can be physically copied at virtually no cost, the economics of software may be different from those of hardware. Some of the system software may be purchased with copyright limitations, while some may be developed for the specific combination of equipment in the cell and its intended uses. Client firms should be able to use the full power of the software system at the facility by paying only a part of its development cost. Even with license restrictions on proprietary software, a client firm may replicate the CAD or the cell hardware in its own factory and be able to negotiate use of the software system with future enhancements at a fraction of the cost it would have to pay on its own.

4. *Sharing Product Technology.* The technology to make particular products can be embodied in software (e.g., data or programs for the cell control computer) or hardware (e.g., special tools or jigs).

The more this technology, which comprises the cell's repertoire, is shared among the client firms, the greater the advantages the facility can provide. Even if the client firms are competitors, they may agree to share general-use product technology as well as system software.

While production economies may be overshadowed by the firms' need to treat product technology as proprietary, sharing may not be precluded, however, since all manner of licensing and subcontracting arrangements are possible. The decisions on sharing product technology among the client firms and between the production and teaching modes of the facility must be decided on a case-by-case basis.

5. *Sharing for Large Companies.*   Large companies are participating or considering participating in small-firm FCIM sharing arrangements for three reasons.

a. *Suppliers of Small Businesses.*   Companies that provide FCIM equipment, software, or materials particularly suited for use in FCIM processes can afford to provide marketing support to a facility that serves multiple small firms more easily than they can afford to work with the firms directly.

b. *Purchasers from Small Businesses.*   Companies that buy parts and components from small firms may participate in establishing shared FCIM facilities to help upgrade or even save their domestic small company sources. Major Department of Defense contractors are interested in the sharing concept because of strategic reasons and to meet various small and disadvantaged business set-aside requirements.

c. *Upgrading Decentralized Operating Components.*   Large companies with decentralized operating components are considering shared centers as an internal service to help the components make automation decisions and economical transitions to FCIM.

It must be emphasized that there is no single best way to achieve these five economies of sharing. Many approaches can be devised that could provide them with different balances, depending on the goals of the facility and those whom it serves.

Part 2: Options for Establishing the FCIM Facility

Determining its primary purpose

Two models. We have assumed that the facility is to be used by its client firms both for production and for educational and training activities. The relationship between the facility and the client firms can fall somewhere along a continuum between two extreme models which we will call:

1. *Profit Center.* Where the facility is treated as a typical, stand alone, business enterprise expected to maximize its return on investment

2. *Service Center.* Where the contribution of the facility is expected to be made through its synergistic contribution to improved performance of the client firms it serves

Under the profit center, effectiveness would be measured by performance against plans, goals, objectives, and budgets, all expressed in terms of the facility itself. It should become profitable at some point, and this objective could be built into management and employee incentive plans. Colleges, universities, and other nonprofit organizations that select this option must be careful to protect their nonprofit status. They must also be alert to charges that they are competing unfairly with companies that must pay taxes and have higher capital costs.

Under the service center, the facility would be more self-effacing for the benefit of the client firms. For example, it might produce small numbers of low-cost but critical parts that would be used by the client firms to create higher value-added products. Alternatively, the facility might operate a high value-added process, providing the backbone for products which the client firms would package for their individual markets. Under this model, the center would be like a catalyst whose value comes from what it allows others to do.

Perhaps the most important factor in deciding where along this continuum to spot the facility will be the types of services the facility is expected to provide. Under the simplest arrangement, the facility could just rent time on the cell and the programming system for each client firm to use as it wishes. At the other extreme, the facility would work interactively with the clients to improve the economics of their operations by helping redesign products for optimum FCIM manufacture, making maximum use of the stored repertoire and efficient production scheduling. If the equipment and software of the center approach the complexity of the cell we have assumed, close interaction may be required to obtain the maximum benefits from sharing.

The future interests of the facility and the client firms should be considered. For example, while the early stages will require teamwork by everybody, the long-term interests of the profit center could be competitive with those of the clients. If the facility charges on a value-added basis rather than just renting time, the work it performs for some client firms will emerge as being relatively more profitable, and this model must be expected to favor the more profitable.

Long-range plans. As long-range plans are developed, they should be compatible with the primary purpose. For example, will the facility be expected to:

1. Add capacity and grow indefinitely as the client firms convert to and rely on it for regular use?
2. Spin off and replace client firms as they develop their own capacities on a scheduled basis?
3. Serve as a standby capacity for peak loads but not regular production after clients develop their own facilities?
4. Provide a continuing basis for developing and testing new technologies and processes, but not sustained production?
5. Schedule itself for extinction by some date when the client firms no longer need it?

Facility policies. What will be the operational relationships between the facility and the client firms? For example:

1. Will the client firms agree to pay for a portion of the facility's capacity or commit to use the facility to help it get started? If so, this form of subsidy would be most consistent with the service center model.
2. Once established, what discretion will the client firms have to use or not use the facility? The greater their sourcing discretion, the more the facility is in competition with other providers including the client firms' own capabilities. Sourcing discretion would be most consistent with the profit center model.
3. Will the facility be allowed to accept or reject work from the client firms? The reverse of the previous question, limiting the right of the facility to choose what it does and whom it serves, would be most consistent with the service center.
4. Will the facility bid for work from the client firms, establishing the price in advance of orders, or will the orders come first, to be followed by fair cost charges? The arm's-length bidding process is consistent with the profit center.
5. Will the facility be allowed to work for other than client firms, and if so, will client firms have priority regardless of profitability to the facility?
6. Will the facility be allowed to set its own pricing strategies (profit center), or will the client firms have a voice in pricing (service center)? Will it simply charge for time used, or will it compute charges for each product it makes? (We are leaving the issue of determining the cost of FCIM-made products to Part 3 and are assuming there is no established market that sets the prices for most of the parts the facility produces.) Three possible strategies might be:

    a. Proportional Pricing.   Where the price is directly related to costs. Under this strategy, the price is set to recover all costs of making the product and may provide for some profit. This could be consistent with the profit center if the facility simply rents time. It could also be consistent with the service center if the client firms share the initial start-up costs, leaving primarily depreciation and current operating costs to be recovered.

    b. Skim Pricing.   Where prices are set high in relation to costs during initial sales to take advantage of customers' willingness to pay a premium for a new product, quality, or service. If the facility can use skim pricing, it may be able to have its early revenues grow faster than capacity use. This strategy would probably be limited to situations where there is no effective market, the market price is significantly higher than the facility's costs, or the client firms are required to use the facility regardless of price. Similar to the value-of-service theory of public utility pricing, this strategy is consistent with the profit center and might allow the facility to charge for short-run setups and educational programs even if their costs are negligible.

    c. Strategic Pricing.   Where prices for initial sales are set low in relation to anticipated long-run costs to build volume, customer acceptance, or dependence. This strategy might be particularly sound for the profit center if client firms are not committed to use the facility. Alternatively, it might be used by the service center if the clients commit to adequate long-term use agreements.

It should be clear that the choice of model will be critical to establishing the type of relationships desired between the facility and client firms. If an arm's-length relationship with operational and pricing independence for the facility is desired, the profit center is indicated. A collaborative relationship of the service center is the other extreme where the value of the facility is measured by its contributions to the client firms, it is transparent to the outside world, and its pricing strategies may not be very important.

    A cooperative relationship could have elements of both. The manager of the facility might have a special commitment to the managers of the client firms but also be measured by the facility's own performance. The balance required by this relationship may be hard to establish and maintain over an extended period unless the economies of sharing reduce costs enough to allow all interests to be satisfied.

Analysis of ownership options

This section discusses factors to consider in deciding who should own the various elements of property that comprise the facility.

The facility itself. Several forms of ownership are possible, with the first choice being whether the facility is a for-profit or nonprofit organization.

1. *A For-Profit Organization.* If the facility will be a for-profit corporation, there will be the question of who owns its stock. The major options are:

   a. *One of the Client Companies.* Perhaps the simplest arrangement would be for the facility to be a wholly owned subsidiary of a client company. This would ease the organizing and fund-raising steps. Appropriate charter, bylaws, and directorship arrangements might be developed to protect the interests of other client firms. But this arrangement would put the entire investment and operating costs of the facility on the books of the single owning firm which would have an interest in early and sustained profitability. While there are ways to limit this effect, it could offset some of the unique advantages of FCIM sharing.

   b. *Several or All of the Client Companies.* Less simple to organize than single-company ownership, this alternative could be consistent with a variety of operating and pricing policies the facility might adopt to benefit the client companies. It would distribute the investment and start-up costs among the client firms, taking full advantage of the financial benefits of sharing. Arrangements might be made to keep ownership within the active group of client firms. Limitations on interlocking directorates and antitrust constraints might present problems.

   c. *Individuals or Other Third Parties.* Depending on the motivations of the owners, this could be a simple arrangement. If their objective is to help the client companies or the affiliated educational institutions, it could be ideal. Some provision might be needed to ensure that shares are not sold by the organizers or their estates to investors who have a short-term profit motive. If the owners intend the facility to be a normal investment for profit, however, pressures may be created that limit operating, pricing, and policy decisions.

2. *A Nonprofit Organization.* The facility might be organized as either a for-profit or nonprofit subsidiary of a nonprofit organization such as an educational institution. This might make it easier to obtain funds from federal, state, local, or other sources, particularly for the educational phase. It might lead to educational discounts for equipment purchases. It could provide ownership stability for an extended period, and allow for orderly disposal if the facility outlives its usefulness. It might lead to tensions over scheduling the facility for production or education. While educa-

tional use could help absorb start-up and overhead costs, it would be wise to avoid the appearance of public subsidy for selected client companies.

Major facility hardware.   The initial hardware components of the facility are assumed to be the manufacturing cell and the CAD computer or programming system. Two options—ownership by the facility or by a third-party leasing firm—can apply to both components. Because of its relatively low cost, the CAD computer or programming system would probably be owned unless it were part of a leased turnkey installation that includes system software.

1. *Facility Ownership.*   The facility might be the owner of the equipment if the owners of the facility are willing to carry the investment on their books. This is most probable if the facility is owned by a nonprofit organization or the client firms. A nonprofit owner of the facility might be able to acquire the hardware at reduced cost through donation or educational discounts. It might be easier to replace the hardware if it is owned by the facility, unless a leaser can provide discounts and has ready markets for used equipment. Facility ownership would prevent maintenance, wear, and damage disputes with a leaser.

2. *Leasing from a Third-Party Owner.*   Leasing the hardware by the facility may provide several advantages. The facility would limits its initial hardware cost to the rental amount without carrying an investment on its books. The lease would be for an agreed period and there might be provision for early termination if, for example, the facility needs to change equipment or is not successful. If the leasing firm specializes in FCIM equipment, it may obtain discounts and be an economical source of advice, software, and other services. If additional cells are anticipated during the term of the lease, the leasing firm might be able to supply them at a lower cost than the facility could arrange.

There may also be tax advantages to the leasing firm that could be passed on in the form of lower rent, but its cost of money may exceed that of a nonprofit organization. The rent, which might be based on actual use or a start-up curve, might be easier to distribute among the client firms than depreciation charges. Under some conditions, leasing the equipment might give the client firms the greatest possible advantage from sharing.

Basic system software.   By basic system software, we mean the programs and data that allow parts to be designed with the CAD computer or programming system and communicated to the cell control computer for manufacture. By ownership, we mean either title to, or licensed rights to use the software. The basic system software may be an integration of several existing packages obtained from multiple sources along with some created specifically for the facility. While some proprietary packages may only be available under license restrictions that would limit possible uses by the client firms, we are assuming that suitable software can be obtained under acceptable terms. Although costs of developing software by a company that will use it internally are normally recorded as expenses on the company's books, the total cost of the basic system software may equal the hardware investment. The three ownership options are:

1. *The Facility Owns.*   The basic system software will probably be subject to continuing improvement and may need to be managed by the facility. Adding features to the software to accommodate new design processes or cell augmentations is a way of increasing the equipment's repertoire and hence its value. This task may be easier if the facility owns the software or obtains the rights to use it as the facility and client firms find most advantageous over time. For example, one firm may establish its own CAD system but continue to use the facility's cell. Another may install a duplicate cell at its own site but continue to use the facility CAD system. Another may establish both but continue to participate in system developments with the facility and update its own system as improvements are made. The facility may even create its own proprietary software that it allows clients and others to use under license.

A primary benefit of FCIM sharing may come from use of the basic system software by client firms at a fraction of what they would pay if they were to develop it independently or obtain it elsewhere. Facility ownership and control would also ensure that client firms could always learn what they need to know about the technology programmed into the software. If the facility owner is a nonprofit organization, its cost of money for creating the software may be lower (because of donations, government funding, nonprofit status, etc.) and educational features may be incorporated that are not in commercial packages. If the facility owner is a for-profit organization, the cost of developing software which it would lease to client firms may be capitalized.

2. *Owned by Hardware Leaser.*   If the facility rents the hardware, it may also rent the basic system software as part of a turnkey installation package. If the leaser is in the turnkey business and can spread the software cost over several installations in addition to our facility, this could multiply the benefits of sharing and become the lowest possible cost approach. As with the equipment investment, the cost could probably be capitalized and spread over a period of use rather than be handled entirely as a start-up charge. If there is a turnkey leaser that agrees to provide a working, integrated system,

the facility may have fewer problems in identifying and correcting malfunctions that may be caused by hardware and software interaction. Arrangements may have to be made for modifications and independent use by client firms.

3. *Owned by Client Firms.*   The client firms might collectively purchase, develop, or obtain rights allowing each of them to use the basic system software at the facility or their own sites. This could provide the clients with the FCIM sharing benefit of multiple use at partial cost while giving each firm latitude to proceed independently in the future. If the firms plan to include proprietary product technology (discussed below) in their basic software systems, this is a way to provide for it from the start. In addition, this option would be useful if the client firms intend to phase down their dependence on the facility.

Product technology.   By this we mean both the instructions needed by the cell control computer and any special tools or auxiliary hardware to make particular products. As with other aspects of FCIM, product technology can involve high start-up and low use costs. Part of the value of the learning capability of FCIM may depend on client firms sharing product technology. On the other hand, the firms may find greater value in treating their product technology as proprietary. Both objectives may be met if a client firm allows others to use its proprietary product technology under license. The advantages to client firms of owning their own basic system of software also apply to product technology.

Some examples

This section shows how some of the bits in previous sections can interact. We start with a base example, then build two more examples by adding factors to show their effects. Their purpose is to show how the variables can be combined to create multiple-win situations. The numbers used are not intended to be realistic and are for illustrative purposes only.

Base example.   Assume that a small to medium-sized firm decides to establish its own CAD-FCIM facility such as those we have been discussing with:

1. A $500,000 system software and $500,000 installation cost, half in each of the first 2 years.

2. A $5,000,000 hardware investment in the second year.

3. Production beginning in the fourth quarter of the second year, with utilization growth limited to 2 hours per day per quarter by the ability of the engineering and manufacturing staffs to develop cell instructions. Full two-shift operation is attained by the end of the fourth year.

Regardless of any other facts, the facility will not see a positive return on its hardware investment until the fourth year and will have a negative cash flow for several more years.

Shared facility.   Next, assume the same system is established by a facility which owns the equipment and serves 20 client firms. Each firm pays 5 percent of the start-up costs as they are incurred and starts using the facility as soon as possible. For $25,000 for each of the first 2 years, each firm gets the rights to use the same software and start-up arrangements that would cost a single firm $500,000 per year. With 20 design teams at work, additional CAD equipment must be obtained. Use of the FCIM cell grows at 8 hours per day per quarter. By early in the third year, the cell is running two full shifts, and at least one additional cell must be installed by the end of that year. Each client firm may earn a profit on the time it buys from almost the beginning, and should have a positive cash flow during the third year.

Leased turnkey installation.   Finally, assume the shared facility leases the same software and hardware from a third party as a turnkey installation. The supplier has produced the $500,000 system software in anticipation of leasing it to 10 users who will each pay $100,000 over 3 years for use rights. If successful, the leaser will receive $1,000,000 for its $500,000 software investment. The leaser agrees to treat our facility as one of the 10 users, so each of our 20 client firms will pay $1667 per year for 3 years to use software that would cost it $500,000 to develop on its own.

If the software is available when the cell is ordered, engineers of the 20 firms could start developing product technology immediately, allowing the cell to operate near capacity shortly after it is installed with no investment on the facility's or the client firms' books.

Expecting to lease at least 10 growing systems, the leaser has obtained discounts from equipment suppliers, so the cell hardware which would cost $5,000,000 a cell if purchased individually actually costs the leaser $4,500,000. This saving, plus tax advantages, cover the leaser's profit and interest charges. Each client firm has an opportunity to put its early conversion to FCIM on a positive cash flow basis during the second year.

Part 3: The FCIM Accounting Problem

The problem

Up to this point, we have alluded to product costs as if they were readily determinable. Unfortunately, this is not quite so.

A simplified explanation. Standard accounting systems operate on annual, quarterly, monthly, and perhaps shorter cycles to perform four primary functions for a company:

1. Relate expenditures to incomes in order to measure changes in inventories and profit or loss

2. Prevent or detect fraud and misappropriation of assets

3. Determine tax liability

4. Help managers make decisions regarding products, prices, and costs to attain successful operations

To perform these functions (in about this order of emphasis), standard accounting practices were developed to identify each expenditure and trace it through to its ultimate effect.

As a general principle, if an expenditure is made to acquire something of short-term benefit, the expenditure is called an expense and is subtracted from the income received during the period in which it is incurred. If an expenditure is for something of tangible and enduring value, it is called an asset and its value is carried into future periods. If the asset is expected to lose value over time or use, the amount of the loss (depreciation) in each period is deducted from the asset and treated as an expense of that period. We ignore inventories and interest costs in this discussion.

The accounting problems of FCIM systems are caused by:

- The way standard accounting practice treats some of the large, early expenditures

- The long delays between the expenditures and the resulting sales

- The way accounting systems treat various types of knowledge

- The difficulty of relating expenditures to specific sales

- The way accounting systems combine current direct costs with apportionments of previous expenditures

- The tendency of accounting systems to ignore other critical information that is not collected in financial terms

These problems are most easily understood by considering a single firm rather than a shared FCIM facility.

Early expenditures. Standard accounting practice requires a company to record, as current expenses, what it spends to develop computer software, program FCIM equipment to make its products, do strategic market analysis, develop new products, train its people, and make other provisions for the future. The effects of expensing these strategic costs are to:

1. Reduce current profits and show the company in a poorer position than it would have been had it not provided for the future

2. Provide an incentive not to modernize

3. Lose track of the strategic costs when they are incurred so there is cross-period subsidization and the true cost of future production is understated

Long delays. Regardless of whether modernization expenditures are treated as investments or expenses, the time lag between outlays and the resulting sales revenue has two effects:

1. The risk of not recovering the expenditures may be large.

2. The cost of capital during the period of negative cash flow becomes important to the point of being one of the largest elements of the cost of modernization. (This is not unique to FCIM. Half of the cost of bringing a new pharmaceutical to market is the cost of money.)

Accounting treatment of knowledge. When a company pays for the research and development necessary to make new products, train its people, or develop a repertoire of computer-encoded production technology, it is investing in knowledge. Because accountants do not know how to measure the value of knowledge, they assign it a value of zero.

An effect of this is illustrated by inventories. Although treated as an asset on a company's books, most managers strive to reduce parts inventories to minimize risk, reduce carrying charges, and apply the just-in-time concept. One way to reduce these inventories is to simply do away with them and keep the knowledge of how to produce the parts in an FCIM computer. When this is done, the repertoire becomes an infinite inventory with no risk or carrying charges, that can produce the parts on demand. On the company's books, the inventory, which was an asset of value, is replaced with the repertoire, which is treated as having no value. Yet we can envision the time when small companies will be bought and sold for the value of their repertoires.

Relating costs to sales. In its early days, accounting was largely a process of relating labor and material costs to particular jobs and to the sales receipts from those jobs. As centralized activities such as purchasing and accounting grew, and more capital equipment was used, these costs were pooled and charged to production through an overhead rate as a percentage of direct labor. Today, with FCIM, direct labor costs have declined almost to the vanishing point and most of the costs are what used to be treated as overhead.

Mixing current direct costs with apportionments of previous expenditures. The typical factory cost accounting system treats labor, material, and depreciation as similar costs. A $10 hourly use charge that is based on a schedule to recover the purchase price of a machine over many months is treated as being equal to $10 worth of material that has not yet been purchased. But for making operating decisions about how to manufacture a product, the two are not comparable at all. The machine was bought and the money is gone. Purchasing material creates a new out-of-pocket cost, while the real cost of using an otherwise idle machine may be negligible. The normal accounting approach overstates the real cost to process something with capital equipment and can lead to buying more expensive, preprocessed material to reduce the use of an already underused machine.

The typical factory cost accounting system also ignores the interest cost of unrecovered money used to buy equipment and put it into use. Thus, by overstating the true cost of processing and understating the continuing cost of idle capacity, accounting systems can lead to wrong cost estimates, wrong decisions on what orders to accept, and mistakes in weighing tradeoffs among processing alternatives.

Accounting experts are currently developing what they call "activity-based accounting," which measures various support costs like accepting an order, purchasing material, stocking material, and shipping and traces them directly to decisions such as the acceptance of an order. This work will help users of FCIM, but some fundamental problems will still remain. These include:

1. Only direct costs such as material are proportional to sales. The start-up costs of preproduction years have no relationship to sales at all. Even though expenditures for computer software, employee training, factory rearrangement, etc., are made to obtain future sales or reduce future costs, they are treated as expenses when incurred because they do not yield tangible assets of readily deter-

minable value. Normal accounting practice does not allow a company to shift its prior year expenses into current accounts.

2. Depreciation may (but need not) be on a straight-line basis. One alternative, widely used for tax purposes, is to use an accelerated schedule where the amount of depreciation charged during the first year is the greatest and declines in subsequent years. Since for FCIM, production and sales are expected to increase over time, this method produces an inverse rather than direct relationship.

3. Another alternative is to charge depreciation on the basis of use, making it more parallel to the direct variable costs. This would be managerially sound, but if this approach is used to calculate profits while accelerated depreciation is used for tax purposes, the minimum income tax provision may come into play.

4. The choice of number of hours of planned use for the system can be as important as the choice of the depreciation schedule. Any formula for computing hourly costs or charging rates has a dollar figure as the numerator and number of hours over which the dollars are to be spread as the denominator. This was discussed above under Capital Equipment.

5. Because defensible choices for depreciating capital investments can vary by an order of magnitude, and prior period strategic costs simply disappear from view, product "cost" is no longer a function of measurement and instead has become a function of company strategy.

6. While major corporations can use complex accounting systems to determine product costs, there is a scale factor that prevents small companies from using similar systems.

7. Finally, the only time when the initial strategic costs and capital investments can be controlled is when the expenditures are being made. Although these expenditures will determine the bulk of a company's product costs for years to come, most accounting systems tend to ignore them and concentrate on later, routine, and repetitive operations that are of decreasing importance.

Other critical information. Advanced manufacturing is becoming increasingly dependent on quantifiable information other than dollars. The measures used in statistical process control, product reliability, tool wear, and short-run setup times are examples of information that may be more important to factory operations than typical cost numbers, yet what they measure has a major effect on costs. Accounting may need to be extended beyond its traditional bounds.

Why this is significant. The importance of the FCIM accounting problem for small businesses can be seen in terms of two of the functions of an accounting system listed earlier.

1. Relate expenditures to incomes in order to measure changes in inventories and profit or loss. We have shown how it is impossible to relate much of the outflow of funds directly to resulting sales. Instead, many actions taken to benefit future operations are treated as current expenses which detract from profit when they are incurred. For firms and managers measured on the basis of their quarter-to-quarter and year-to-year profitability, this can provide a strong incentive not to undertake FCIM systems. Further, it may be hard to prevent allowing the initial years that bore the start-up costs from subsidizing future years. As sales and expenses are reported in normal financial statements, a company may appear profitable shortly after its sales of FCIM manufactured products take off, but on a cumulative cash flow basis, the break-even point is probably much later. Because of subsidization by the start-up years, a company could appear to run at an indicated profit each year after start-up costs have been written off, but never reach the cash flow break-even point before the system is scrapped.

2. Help managers make decisions regarding products, prices, and costs to attain successful operations. So far, we have been primarily discussing sales and total costs of a company using an FCIM system, but operating decisions are made for individual jobs or increments— not the totals. In simpler times, records for each job would show profit or loss by the customer, job type, or individual job. From this information, sound decisions could be made on what work to seek and how to control costs.

A prime advantage of an FCIM system is its ability to produce short runs of many different parts. But if each run is a sale, how does a company determine what orders to accept and what price to charge to yield a desired profit if it can't determine its cost to make the run? Further, while each initial run of a product involves preparatory work that need not be done for subsequent runs, how does a firm estimate the number of production runs to use as the basis for spreading the preparatory costs? How does it decide what new products to make or choose its mix of new products and repeat runs?

At this point, the implications of the FCIM accounting problem for government procurement should be fairly clear. What sort of negotiations and subsequent audit can lead to a fair distribution of costs among products made for the government and private sector customers? If it is hard for a company to determine its costs for its own purposes, how will it ever be able to reach agreement on the cost of sales to the government?

Some possible accommodations

The advantage of shared FCIM facilities. In previous sections, we have explained several ways a group of client firms can share start-up costs. While by no means solving the accounting problem, sharing may reduce the impact of these costs for each firm, thus reducing the significance of the problem. If it is assumed that start-up costs will be spread among 20 client firms equally, each would absorb 5 percent of most of these costs (except for education and training time for their own people). For this amount, each firm would obtain approximately the same value that the single firm would receive if it went alone. For all practical purposes, the start-up costs may become small enough to be ignored by the client firms. Not a solution but an accommodation.

Controllable versus contingent cost drivers. The term "cost driver" is increasingly popular in accounting literature. The idea is to identify the activities that cost money with greater accuracy and sensitivity to cause and effect. While not wanting to take issue with or repeat what has been written, we believe that the importance of start-up costs to the success of an FCIM system is not receiving adequate attention. Start-up cost drivers can be divided into two categories:

1. Controllable cost drivers—individual activities or decisions that lead directly to planned expenditures

2. Contingent cost drivers—the interaction, often delayed, among several actions or decisions that lead to unexpected costs

Ordering a piece of equipment is a controllable cost driver, as is ordering software to use with it. Finding that the equipment and software are not compatible and the subsequent actions taken to recover from the unanticipated problem are contingent cost drivers.

The concept of "contingent costs"—a thought normally restricted to expenses such as bad debts in most accounting texts—may be important when establishing FCIM systems. To be successful, these systems require people and organizations to do right the first time, things they may have not done before. A single, runaway contingent driver can increase the cost of the FCIM system to the point where it may never be profitable. By the time traditional accounting reports indicate the problem, most of the damage will already have been done.

In order to examine this concept, we developed an FCIM systems planning chart that shows 43 events—from writing the initial concept paper to completing the first production batch. The events are organized in five streams of activity for Marketing, Product Design, CAD/CAM and Process Control Systems, FCIM Equipment, and the Facility. Twenty of these events are controllable cost drivers, but of the 20, only 6 are directly related to making a specific product.

An additional 5 events, where different lines of activity come together for testing, are identified as contingent cost drivers. If work up to these points has been done well, the tests will be almost cost-free. But if mistakes have been made, these are the points where problems will be most likely to surface. Because they are not routine, companies find the costs produced by these contingent drivers are difficult to predict and control.

Companies might formally budget amounts for each of the contingent cost drivers they can identify. This would underscore the contingency aspect of the possible costs, and just thinking about them may lead to actions that minimize them.

The dual-path P&L statement. The two primary displays that companies use to show their financial condition are the balance sheet and the profit and loss statement. The balance sheet is a static snapshot of a company's position at a specific time, while the P&L statement is a summary of operations during a period of time. Accounting convention requires changes in the earned surplus line of consecutive balance sheets to be linked by the P&L statement for the intervening period.

This convention was developed when company outlays tended to fall into the two relatively neat categories of (1) provision for the future or investment and (2) current operations or expense. In simpler times, investment or provision for the future normally yielded something tangible and durable like a machine or building while expensed items were consumed during the period. Since then, the test for treating an expenditure as an operational expense or an investment has come to be based on the tangible or durable aspect more than the reason for making the expenditure.

Some expenditures, particularly for research and development or employee training, have long presented an accounting problem. The objective was clearly provision for the future, but since knowledge and capability are not tangible, there was usually no result to call an asset. The problem was handled two ways. First, in even the most progressive companies, these expenditures were usually modest in relation to overall operations and they tended to occur at a relatively constant rate so they were not much of an issue. Second, providing for the future was viewed as a continuing operational requirement for staying in business—thus the problem was defined away. Over time, the performance of companies with continuing R&D and training programs tended to be recognized by the investment community, and they were often accorded higher price-earnings ratios for their stocks.

Today, more than ever before, companies must develop new technology or create manufacturing capabilities that require a surge in outlays which accounting conventions treat as a current expense. These provision-for-the-future expenses become merged with routine operating expenses on the P&L statement in the single path that leads from Sales to Changes in Earned Surplus. A bold program for the future can thus appear the same as mismanagement. The accounting conventions, intended to provide a conservative view of the company, when coupled with the normal P&L statement, become a perverse measure and an incentive not to modernize.

The dual-path P&L splits the statement in two, showing one path for routine operating expenses and a second path for the uncapitalized costs of providing for the future, or what we call strategic costs. Both paths appear side by side and lead to a common bottom line. A P&L statement organized this way would provide a more useful display of information with minimal changes to accounting conventions. While companies may provide some of this information in text or footnotes today, it does not have the same effect as two parallel columns of figures would have. Few analysts, for example, routinely calculate two P/E ratios, one for current operations and one for the long term, as the dual paths would almost demand.

Managers could be measured against one set of criteria for their performance on the operating side and a different set on the provision-for-the-future side. Bonuses, promotions, stock options, and retirements could be designed to take the two paths into account and support both short-term profitability and long-term strategic objectives.

There is no reason why the strategic cost path must include only expenses. For example, a significant inventory reduction and sale of the space formerly used to contain it may produce a one-time positive cash flow which could also be reported in this path rather than in the routine operations path. The future year reductions in inventory carrying costs and lower space costs would, of course, be shown in the operations path when they occur.

Over time, the strategic costs path can lead to an indication of how well a company manages its technology. There ought to be a positive correlation between these costs and relatively healthy future operations data.

This is not a general solution to the problems of justifying and measuring investments in technology. The dual-path P&L may be subject to manipulation and it may even be fraud-prone. But some form of it, even as a supplemental statement, may be a step forward that could be taken without costly changes in accounting principles or systems. For a shared FCIM system, the facility could show the strategic costs that it bills to client firms as distinct from current period operating expenses. This would allow the client firms to show the expenses on the appropriate paths of their own P&L statements.

Cumulative cash flow accounting. Several people are working on an idea based on cumulative cash flow that may provide small companies with a watershed opportunity to simplify their accounting problem. If, as we believe, accounting has become more a function of strategy than a measurement, the strategic plan or multiyear budget of a company may be the best basis for evaluation.

Under this notion, only two sets of numbers really matter from an operating management standpoint—the cumulative outlays and the cumulative receipts. Concentrating on these two numbers and how decisions affect them would show whether a company is doing what it undertook to do in the same way a lender looks at the company.

To illustrate this idea, when a company decides to convert to FCIM, whether by itself or using a shared facility, it would make a cumulative cash flow projection for several years. This projection would show the planned cumulative outlays, receipts, interest costs, and profit by the end of the projected period—let's say 5 years. As the company makes start-up expenditures, it would relate the cumulative outlays, the passage of time, and what is accomplished to the projection. As production starts and sales begin, the cash flow effects would be compared to the plan.

During any period, if the accomplishments and the net cash flow are on target, the company would have attained the anticipated profit. A variance between the anticipated net cash flow position and accomplishments would be shown as a profit or loss.

This idea is preliminary and has weaknesses. It will not satisfy all requirements for an accounting system. But it may be useful for guiding the internal operating decisions of a small company. It is an example of the type of accounting innovation that may have to precede successful use of FCIM by small U.S. companies.

Conclusion. Current accounting practices are having a negative impact on the ability of small companies to justify moving to advanced manufacturing, obtain adequate financing for the move, conduct their business, operate modern processes effectively, and do business with the Department of Defense. This serious condition requires national attention. But until accounting practices are modernized to meet the new realities, shared facilities that help small companies make the transition to advanced manufacturing may have to include help in understanding the limitations of current accounting practices, and provide assistance in augmenting typical accounting systems.

The IPK-Berlin Institute as a Model of the Fraunhofer Society in Germany

Prof. Dr. h. c. mult. Dr-Ing. Günter Spur and Rita Pokorny, MA

Production Technology Center
Berlin, Germany

Introduction and Background

In 1976, a cooperation contract was signed between the Institute for Machine Tools and Production Technology of the Technical University of Berlin (IWF), founded in 1904, and the Fraunhofer Institute for Production Systems and Design Technology (IPK). Thus basic and applied research in the development of future-oriented technologies were combined; since 1986 they have been in one building under the name Production Technology Center (PTZ).

The Institute for Machine Tools and Manufacturing Technology (IWF) is responsible for basic research and instruction. The combination of research and practical application with academic teaching provides for the swift flow of the latest findings into lecture halls and areas of practice. Project work and master's dissertations are produced in direct relation to research projects, and undergraduate students have the opportunity of working on daily industrial-based projects as research assistants. Training programs and seminars for clients from industry represent another form of conveying the latest technical production know-how. Moreover, young engineers from production technical companies and from foreign research institutes have the possibility of working on basic research over a determined period of time. Another major focus of the two institutes is cooperation with small and medium-sized companies. These companies are offered support in problem solving and are aided in attaining the support of government sponsoring.

One of the tasks of the Fraunhofer Institute for Production Systems and Design Technology is the technology transfer of fundamental innovations in functional applications to industrial and public contractors through applied research and development. Technology transfer is therefore not limited to the initiation of principle and feasibility studies but above all consists of practical development work and analysis for the contractors. Depending on the task, work can result in program systems, hardware solutions, or detailed planning documents, including testing in the laboratories.

The goal behind these activities is to contribute toward the further development of the "factory of the future." Therefore, research at the Production Technology Center includes, along with solutions of specific tasks, the background of aspired computer integrated factory operation and modern production technology.

Historical Background

Founded in 1949, the Fraunhofer Society (Fraunhofer Gesellschaft) has expanded drastically and now incorporates 47 institutes and independent working teams and has established its reputation as a trendsetter in translating scientific findings into user-oriented results for industrial application. The society, which chose its name to honor the glasscutter and practice-oriented scientist Josef von Fraunhofer (1787–1826), is a nonprofit organization employing more than 7000 people. Their respective institutes carry out projects for the benefit of the government and industry on the basis of covering the expenses.

In comparison with similar institutes in other countries, the Fraunhofer Society developed rather slowly to its present size and variety of scientific spectrum. This has proved characteristic of the historic development of applied research in this country.

By the end of the nineteenth century the impetus for a collaboration between science and industry was instigated mainly by the progressive and expanding branches of electrotechnology, the chemical industry, and machine tool engineering. This cooperation largely depended on individuals via the promotion of scientifically or technologically trained entrepreneurs. The development was furthered by an intensive and focused state support for the industries and sciences, while guaranteeing for the time being their status of individual orientation.

This is the background against which the foundation of the professorship for machine tools and manufacturing technology should be considered. It was founded at the Königlich-Technische Hochschule

Berlin-Charlottenburg in 1904 under the directorship of Prof. Georg Schlesinger. Two years later the professorship of machine tools and industrial economics at Aachen set another example of the major importance being attached to the systematic improvement of manufacturing methods and production efficiency by the state. It was at that time that universities discovered the factory as a scientific field of research.

Schlesinger was an expert in rationalization. His views on the direction of scientific research carried out in institutes directly toward the shop floor level left their imprint on all German chairs for production technology from then on. This commonly shared attitude of industry-driven production technological research at the universities was confirmed in 1937 when the "Hochschulgruppe Fertigungstechnik" (Academic Society of Manufacturing Technology) was founded. This shows the direct genealogical line from Fraunhofer to Schlesinger and his colleagues to follow. All of them could have legitimately given their names to the Fraunhofer Society. During his life span Schlesinger made an effort to free theoretical sciences from their ivory tower by favoring the know-how, material, and personnel transfer between industry and university on both a national and an international level. He was not only a scientist and pedagogue but also a gifted inventor, design engineer, and contractor. Additionally, he worked as a consultant and advisor to the major German industrial associations and public committees.

Schlesinger also took the first step toward the introduction of contract research, which nowadays is a characteristic working method at the Fraunhofer Society. These proceedings were made possible by the relative autonomy of the university administration. The industry on its side provided the equipment for research laboratories and made basic research possible. It profited by taking over the innovations developed by the institute.

One of Schlesinger's major interests was directed toward the American research for the rationalization of the factory. At a very early stage he contacted Hugo Münsterberg, a Harvard psychology professor and former student of Wilhelm Wundt, to try to apply his empirical findings in the field of labor rationalization to German standards. On Schlesinger's initiative a professorship of psychotechnology was established at the Berliner Technische Hochschule in 1918. This institute developed into the present institute for sciences of labor. It was another American model that marked Schlesinger's commitment to the introduction of modern production methods in the automobile industry.

Being Jewish, Schlesinger was forced to emigrate in 1933. Before leaving Germany, however, Schlesinger was able to recommend Otto

Kienzle as his successor. The latter received the professorship in 1934. The professorate was now called "Lehrstuhl für Betriebswirtschaft und Werkzeugmaschinen" (Chair for Industrial Economy and Machine Tools).

Under the regime of the national socialists the Berlin institute was obliged to carry out armament research. The end of World War II left the institute widely destroyed. Nevertheless the Technische Hochschule was reopened in 1946 as Technische Universität Berlin (TUB). The curriculum for engineering students was supplemented by a strong humanities faculty.

The Department of Machine Tools and Manufacturing Technology also entered the phase of reconstruction. In 1965, Günter Spur was called to take over the chair. Under his directorship the institute developed into a research center of international reputation. In close collaboration with the TUB professorship of automation, founded in 1964 under the directorate of Prof. Wilhelm Simon, numerous important projects in the field of manufacturing technological automation were carried out with the participation of industrial partners. Following Simon's death, his field of activities was integrated into the Institute of Machine Tools and Manufacturing Technology.

The constant increase of industrial projects at the institute brought to light several deficiencies in the structure of the university administration. An adequate employment of personnel and financial means in the project was very complicated according to bureaucratic administrative rules. As a consequence Spur suggested the foundation of an additional research institute along with the university institute. Its organization is structured in such a way that it allows a flexible adaptation to the needs of the customers while at the same time ensuring a mutual collaboration with the university institute.

This proposition was met when a commission acting on behalf of the government, which had started an initiative to support industry in Berlin, recommended the foundation of a Fraunhofer Institute. On the day of its foundation in 1976, the Fraunhofer Institute for Production Systems and Manufacturing Technology (IPK Berlin) established a cooperation agreement with the university institute which provided the scientific-technological collaboration. This agreement also secured the need for laboratory space and equipment.

The twin institute found a home in the Produktionstechnisches Zentrum (Production Technology Center) in 1986. It represents a rare symbiosis of academic basic research, practice-oriented contract research, and undergraduate and postgraduate tutoring. All these activities are carried out under the heading of interdisciplinary cooperation. In addition, both institutes work in the fields of further education and international transfer of know-how.

Development and Corporate Identity
of the Fraunhofer Society

Although applied and contract-oriented research has been widely accepted since the end of World War II, this sector never managed to reach the status of the independent basic research carried out at universities and other state-sponsored institutions (e.g., Kaiser-Wilhelm-Gesellschaft, now Max-Planck-Gesellschaft). When the Fraunhofer Society was founded, the term "contract research" was nearly unknown. As a consequence the expression "industry-related research" was coined, a widening of the term "applied research" and in opposition to state-sponsored theoretical sciences.

The crystallization of the present concept of the Fraunhofer Society is the result of a long-term positioning process in the German research world. It was formed by the discussions about ensuring a financially secure society by public basic funding and about the exchanges of opinion on the limits exercised by the government.

The self-definition process was further influenced by the necessity of defining the society against existing research societies and academic research in general. The strongest influence on the Fraunhofer concept, however, was exercised by the definite demand in the economy for research accomplishments in the joint field of science and technology.

The initial phase in the development of the Fraunhofer Society includes the postwar years until 1954, when the society was established as an association with a strongly regional focus on Bavaria. At that time the society worked as an organization which procured commissions and research funds to "single researchers." The funds transmitted by the Fraunhofer Society came to a large extent from public enterprises—the greater part of it from the European Recovery Program—only a small amount of private finances were involved. The fact that the funds were committed led to the dilemma that the necessary pilot research was not financially covered in an adequate way.

The Bundesforschungsministerium (Federal Research Ministry) only hesitantly committed itself to the society partly because of its pronounced orientation toward industry, which seemed to government officials an uncomfortable competitor to existing research institutions. Only a few firms consented to place orders consistently. Advance payment for the research commissions was avoided when possible, a fact which implied that the society's liquidity was not at its best. Up to the present day industrial financing of academic or nonacademic research is not common practice in Germany.

A change was brought about for the Fraunhofer Society in the mid-1950s. The society began establishing its own institutes which directly carried out contract research for industry and the Verteidigungsministerium (Defense Department). At the same time the Wirt-schaftsministerium (Department of Trade and Industry) of Bavaria and Baden-Württemberg started basic financing programs for the Fraunhofer Society to secure its survival.

In the years up to 1959 a total of 14 institutes were founded, four of which were dedicated to defense research. Along with the institutes, a patent office was founded in 1953 which has the duty to support the counseling, application, maintenance, and exploitation of inventions which are of economic interest and to further the contacts between the inventor and interested parties from industry.

In Germany statistical inquiries of patent data form an important basis to the early detection of technological trends. The contribution of the Fraunhofer Society to this field consists of the documentation and evaluation—in collaboration with the Munich Institute for Economy Research—of major technological inventions. The consequent analyses, evaluation, and prognosis are carried out to determine the international competitiveness of certain fields.

The rules of business procedures are arranged in such a way that a patent-qualified invention being made at the institute during work on an industrial project will automatically be owned by the enterprise in question. If the industrial partner shows no interest in the invention, the Fraunhofer Society has the right to apply for a patent and to exploit the invention. In any case the society obtains the ordinary right of using the invention for its own purposes. However, it is not transferable. The inventor or inventor team will be reimbursed according to the law of employee-inventor reimbursement. Should neither the customer nor the Fraunhofer Society claim a right to the invention, inventors are free to have the invention patented at their own expense.

If state authorities partly finance an industrial project, in some cases the partner from industry has to be prepared for possible restrictions to the newly acquired right. It may be agreed that the partner be granted only an ordinary right of use. This implies the Fraunhofer Society can sell the right of use to other firms as well. Experience has proved that intellectual and economical rights of the inventor have been met while the efficient application in both the field of research and industrial practice was secured at the same time.

Also in the 1960s pilot research projects were forced to work on insufficient financial means, which were drawn from the federal state's budget, private donations, and sporadic subsidies. This deficiency induced the managing board of the Fraunhofer Society to increase its efforts to bring about an acceptable concept of additional state financing. In 1969, the Fraunhofer Society was finally acknowledged as a public institution, which implied its institutional funding by federal means in the shape of annually increasing basic allowances. This change of status gave rise to the expansion of the Fraunhofer Society as an applied research institution between 1969 and 1979.

The foundation for the Fraunhofer Society's specific financing concept, however, was laid in 1973 by a government cabinet resolution, which was put into action in 1975. This resolution marks a change in government evaluation of contract research as opposed to 1971 when a team of experts critically pointed out the small scale of contract research in German research capacity compared to international standards. The relatively low financial support granted by the state and industry for this sector was also criticized. Regarding the future of the Fraunhofer Society, its task in furthering the share of contract research in Germany was pointed out. At the same time the society was expected to carry out user-oriented research in the fields of preparatory contract research as well as project-related investigations subsequent to its achieved results.

The central idea of the Fraunhofer model is designed in such a way that the institutional subsidies, consisting of 90 percent given by the Bundesministerium für Forschung und Technologie (Department of Research and Technology) and 10 percent by the Federal Research Ministries is measured against the amount of the remaining, freely acquired financial means. This success-dependent contingent of the basic financing may in general not exceed the 40 percent limit of the total financing volume. The high amount of state research subsidies for industry-related research in Germany is being justified by the argument that a number of highly important research projects—such as the development of new key technologies—would surcharge the efficiency and risk disposition of private enterprises. Moreover, the specific structural disadvantages of small and medium-sized enterprises are to be compensated and the industrial tendency toward the concentration of companies should be counterbalanced. Besides, the state considers itself responsible for securing the competitiveness of German enterprises in the market when compared with research-sponsoring practices for industries in other nations.

The above financing concept represents a compromise between enterprising autonomy and a basic state subsidizing system. It has proved to be a successful financing method for contract research over the years, since it plays the role of an efficiency barometer and success indicator at the same time.

Every 5 years the efficiency of the concept is checked by the state. The share of basic financing shows a falling tendency when considering all Fraunhofer institutes: In the time span from 1974 to 1980, it has dropped from 52 to 39 percent while at the same time the total output of the society tripled (Fig. 6.1). At present, the share of basic financing lies noticeably beyond the 30 percent rate (Fig. 6.2).

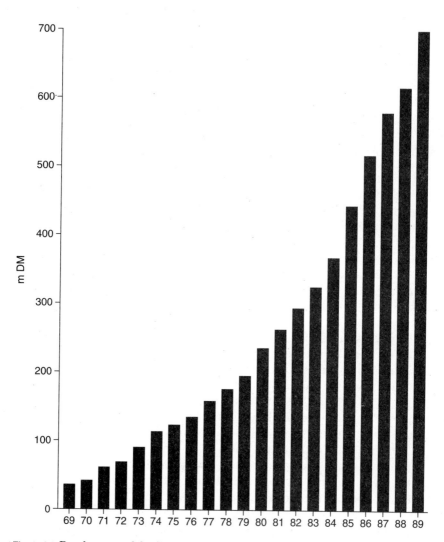

Figure 6.1 Development of the financial volume, 1969–1989.

In contrast, the share of commissions acquired from industry constantly rose. At specifically industry-oriented institutes it sums up to more than 40 percent. The remaining financial needs are covered by means of public research projects. The allowance is granted by the Deutsche Forschungsgesellschaft (German Research Society), the project representatives of the Bundesministerium für Forschung und Technologie (Department of Research and Technology), as well as other public departments which sponsor joint projects between institutes and industry.

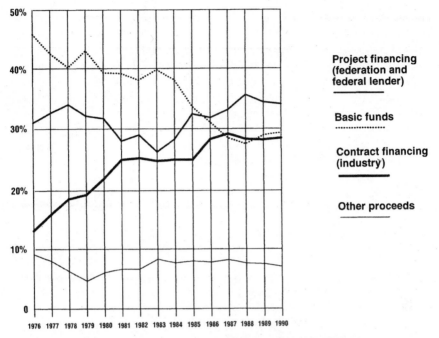

Figure 6.2 Relative financing of division contract research, 1976–1990.

There are two ways in which the cooperation between the Fraunhofer institutes and industry may take place: by the joint participation of several institutes and enterprises in compound projects in a precompetitive mode, and by contract research for an enterprise. In the field of compound research the Fraunhofer Institute takes part either as an initiator and "prime contractor" or as a partner. The cooperating industrial firms are usually enterprises which are on one hand dependent on the development of key technologies; on the other hand, however, they cannot afford to take the high financial risk of long-term research. This is why compound projects are state-funded. Within the last years the amount of compound projects financed by the European Community (EC) and those in which the Fraunhofer Society has participated have risen greatly.

The following criteria are used to choose projects that are sponsored:

- The project partners (firms and institutes) have to be EC-based.

- The results of research are to strengthen the technical know-how of European firms against non-European competitors.

- The results lead to a balance of performance in several European regions.

The EC usually subsidizes 50 percent of the research partners' respective financial expenditures. In special cases like feasibility studies the EC fully covers the expenses. The Fraunhofer Society attaches great importance to supportive cooperation with small and medium-sized enterprises. In a country with extremely high wages these enterprises are constantly confronted with the demand of producing high-quality products, while at the same time trying to lower the costs through rationalization.

This situation increases the demand for expert knowledge on each level of the enterprising activity. A small enterprise, however, cannot afford to employ specialists for every problem field, a fact which implies that it needs external help.

To meet these demands the Fraunhofer Society developed a package of graded measures to provide flexible transfer of know-how:

- Technological information and counseling

- Cooperation in projects with the special financial sponsorship of the ERP (European Recovery Program, previously Marshall Plan) and by AIF (Arbeitsgemeinschaft Industrielle Forschungsvereinigung) (Society of Industrial Research Associations) supported by the Bundesministerium für Wirtschaft (Department of Trade and Commerce)

- Collaboration sponsored by federal funds

In addition, the Fraunhofer Society has a special fund at its disposal. This fund was raised by the Bundesministerium für Forschung und Technologie (Department of Research and Technology) and it is specifically directed toward cooperation with the described firms. On one hand the performance of the Fraunhofer Institute in a firm may be subsidized by this fund (40 to 60 percent of the order value); on the other hand these means may cover the costs of an internal industry project, provided it serves the acquisition of necessary fundamental findings which may at some stage of R&D investigation be applied to small and medium-sized enterprises. This specific program has at present an annual funding of 5 million DM.

With the transition to the European Single Market in 1993 small and medium-sized enterprises will have to meet the challenge of a huge common market. These enterprises in particular need support to secure their competitiveness. The institutes of the Fraunhofer Society support these firms in their enterprising reorientation, their adaptation of new projects and procedures to the changed standards, and their search for cooperation partners.

The Fraunhofer Society focuses on an intensive collaboration with the universities. This is why in many cases the Fraunhofer Society shares the same building with the corresponding university institute. The Berlin twin institute is headed by a scientist who is at the same time an academic teacher, the director of the university institute concerned, and the manager of the cooperating Fraunhofer institute.

The collaboration of the two institutes results in the following mutual advantages:

For the Fraunhofer Society:

- Access to the results of basic research
- Recruitment of young scientists
- Collaboration of students in research projects
- Postgraduate training and teaching possibilities for academic staff of the Fraunhofer institute

For the university:

- Cooperation in science-oriented projects
- Additional jobs for undergraduates
- Integration of practice-oriented results of research into academic teaching
- Making use of administrative services of the Fraunhofer Society

For university and Fraunhofer institute likewise:

- Attractive conditions for the joint nomination of executive managers
- Formation of joint interdisciplinary research fields
- Joint usage of scientific-technological equipment

Each of the 47 Fraunhofer institutes defines itself as an autonomous enterprising institution, as an independently planning nonprofit enterprise, which shapes its own scientific and economic concerns (Fig. 6.3 shows the various fields of research at the institutes and the number of employees). The acquisition of projects takes place within the institutions and orients itself by the principle of acquiring as high as possible a share in direct industrial projects. The institutes' management is free to decide on the choice, the order, the realization, and the financing of the research assignments.

An advisory council consisting of renowned personalities from the world of industry, research, and administration is at the disposal of each institute. In the long run research activities of the Fraunhofer institutes are determined by the various interests of the client as

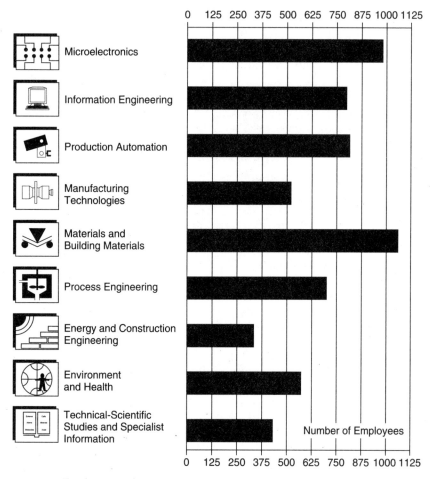

Figure 6.3   Employees in the sectors of research, 1990.

well as the amount of financial means agreed upon in the projects. In more than half of its R&D activities, the Fraunhofer Society concentrates on the solution of acute industry-technological problems, which demand a maximum period of development of 5 years. This is why the activities are funded up to 50 percent by industrial means. The second area comprises the development of future key technologies for industry. Those projects are funded by the state because of their high technological and industrial risk on one hand and the longer duration of development, up to 10 years, on the other.

Eventually, some institutes of the Fraunhofer Society contribute to the establishment of federal preventive activities in the field of environment protection. In this case as well the public project funds provide the biggest part in financing; however, a rise in the participation of industry is noticeable.

The various Fraunhofer institutes are supported by a central administration office in the fields of financial planning, personnel matters of contract building, and construction, as well as accountancy and procurements. To enable this central office to cope with the above administrative and managing-economic tasks, it has been equipped with an overall electronic information system containing all the relevant data on a decentralized basis which also assists in carrying out cost controlling.

Each Fraunhofer institute is expected to guarantee within its business context the fulfillment of the society's statutes: The Fraunhofer Society for the funding of applied research is a nonprofit, tax-privileged society acknowledged by the tax office.

The society is bound by commercial accountancy, according to the German code of commerce. The tax privileges enjoyed by the society imply exemption from corporation tax, trade tax, and property tax. It may further sign donation certificates for endowments given to the society and its institutes. In addition to that, the value-added tax is halved.

The Fraunhofer Society is supervised by a board of surveyors as well as the society's senate. This senate shares among other things the responsibility of important strategy planning. It is constituted of renowned public representatives. The managing board of the Fraunhofer Society is supported by a technological council, consisting of the directors and one academic staff representative of the institutes.

The transfer of know-how into the economy is executed by the institutes partly within the context of industry projects and partly by a series of diverging qualification and advanced training events. Conferences are held regularly on an international basis alongside special topic seminars. Those activities meet the interest of specific target groups in firms, unions, and staff committees. The various institutes appreciate the changing of staff members to jobs in industry since they consider it an especially successful example of technology transfer.

Research Activities at the Twin Institute IWF/IPK

The twin institute's activities are dedicated to the constant upgrading of the manufacturing technology. They deal with all the important development potential in current production technology and are characterized by a constant attempt to transmit the result of scientific research into practical usage in the industrial context. This implies a constant search for new paths, options, and possibilities to increase the efficiency of innovative actions within the economy. The technology of manufacturing processes has provided an important basis for the further development of production technology. Research activities were above all directed to the application of new cutting-tool materials, the processing of new materials, as well as the numerical modeling and technological optimization of manufacturing processes.

In the 1980s a series of research projects marked the twin institute's swift reaction to the expanding development in cutting-tool material technology. A particular stress was laid on the investigation of the influence of the grinding wheel structure of corundum and CBN grinding wheels and its behavior during application.

In the field of cutting with geometrically defined cutting processes, attention was focused on the material of coated polycrystalline diamonds (PCDs). The tests cover the whole spectrum of PCD machining from grinding and electrical discharge erosives cutting to the application of the polycrystalline diamond as a cutting tool, and in the case of cutting PCD the further development and adaptability of continuous conditioning procedures such as jet and plunge conditioning. The investigations concerning the application of this cutting-tool material led to a geometrically optimized design of PCD cutting indexible inserts.

Within the last years, machine tool development of coated cutting-tool materials has gradually come into the field of vision. An early stage of the research proved the advantages of this tool for the machining of highly ductile materials. In addition to that, future-oriented investigations concerning the internal thread production by thread drilling and thread rolling have been carried out.

The problems concerning production technology cannot be solved, however, without the consideration of aspects of material technology. Especially when machining fiber-reinforced plastics (FRPs), ceramics, and monocrystalline silicon, damage of areas close to the surface plays a more important role than is the case with conventional materials. High cutting temperatures frequently cause burning and decomposition of FRP and may in some cases affect the electrical properties of silicon. In this field as well a series of research activities have resulted in future-oriented developments.

In the area of ceramic machining the institute cooperates with many industrial firms, especially with machine tool, ceramic, and cutting-wheel producing companies. The development of continuous in-process dressing of diamond cutting for the reduction of surface layer damage of ceramic components and the finding of ceramic-specific material removal mechanisms are to be pointed out. For turning of FRP a method for infrared thermographical finding of cutting temperatures has been developed. This result is expected to give new impulses to cutting research for metal and ceramics as well as drilling and milling operations. In 1987, an industrial workshop, Machining of Ceramics, was founded, which consists of 36 national and international firms. An additional workshop was founded in 1989, this time consisting of 14 firms.

It is a tradition that the investigation and development of manufacturing procedures constitute a focus in the manufacturing department. This includes major results, which were achieved in the 1960s in the area of difficult cutting property materials such as highly alloyed steels in thermal cutting. It was at this time that investigations concerning the original zone of chip division by interrupting the cutting process during plastic turning were carried out. They contributed mainly to the clarification of chip formation.

In the field of cutting with geometrically undefined cutting conditions attention was also focused on the work concerning lapping. In this case, new kinematic process-control strategies were elaborated for industrial use by developing a model of the complex kinematics of the lapping process.

As a conceptual basis of complex machining systems, an extensive analysis of rotation-oriented workpiece-spectrum parts was carried out in the 1980s by commission of a well-known firm. The information about maximum parts measurement as well as the machining jobs necessary for the manufacturing of form elements could be derived from the specification of form elements. Stored in a databank on the basis of these findings, parts containing all the form elements of the analyzed workpiece were theoretically designed. They further allow for a checkup of the machine concept with the help of machining simulation.

The above investigations led to the development of machine-tool concepts while taking into account the equal integration of various machining technologies, new lathe concepts for complete machining, as well as flexible clamping devices. In addition, the innovative concept for a numerically controlled multispindle turning center was set up in collaboration with another firm. It has since been realized as a prototype and has been presented on the major European machine tool exhibitions.

In the field of clamping technology the institute developed a compensated clamping device using quartz-crystal ceramics as a clamping or compensating element. A sensor for surveillance of the clamping power in conventional powerful chucking is currently being patented.

The integration of NC machine tools and workpiece and worktool handling marked the dominating points of discussion in the 1970s. The expression "manufacturing cell" was coined at the institute to describe the degree of autonomy of a unit in manufacturing technology. Numerous solutions developed in the course of industrial compound projects marked important steps for developments in machine tool manufacturing since they furthered the idea of integration and development of machine modules. The present level of research of flexible manufacturing systems as well as the development in accuracy determining machine components made of new materials such as main spindles from fiber-reinforced plastics and advanced engineering ceramics are to some extent due to the institute's collaboration. In addition to the optimization of modules new machine concepts and advanced machining systems have been developed.

As early as 1974 the industrial robot was investigated as an automation device. In addition to their first practical application for handling heavyweight and hot machine tools (picture tube manufacturing) research projects concerning the constructive and control-technological improvement of industrial robots were launched. An advanced control system for point-to-point (PTP) and contour-controlled robots was the result of a long-term collaboration with leading firms. This was the basis for the technological and economic success of the industrial robot. At present the automobile industry in particular applies machines which were conceived during this phase of collaboration.

Off-line programming and sensor integration are further activities carried out at the institute. The specific demands of medium-sized enterprises, due to their broad spectrum of application, were covered by a low-cost control for handling devices. Up to 12 axes can be programmed in a PTP operation. At present, considerable technology transfer takes place toward the material handling sector for employment in orbital stations and in offshore oil rigs, e.g., the inspection of underwater supporting pillars.

In the 1980s a new methodology for the increasingly complicated programming of NC machine tools was planned. On one hand, the qualified machine user was to be given a greater range of action; on the other hand, the demand of a realistic NC programming checkup was to be considered. A programming and simulation system for turning operations and complete machining was developed. It is integrated into the NC machine and allows a process-simultaneous operation. This programming and simulation system was developed into a stand-alone system and is extensively used in vocational training.

The EC-funded programs ESPRIT and BRITE EURAM incorporate know-how and experience concerning the development of CAD systems, to which well-known German firms have contributed. The possibilities of off-line programming with CAD systems were investigated for the shipping industry. Another firm commissioned the research of knowledge-based systems for tool configuration.

The development of CAD systems led to results which were also used for industrial choice and introduction counseling. More than 50 design offices were analyzed and advice was given concerning the use of CAD systems.

Research in technology is at present accompanied by the skill of the people and a degree of acceptance by those using the results, a problem which calls for a didactic knowledge transfer concerning new research results. It is thus necessary not only to further the technology transfer but also to sponsor the education and training concerning these innovations within a corporate culture.

The above-described technology and training context gave rise to a close collaboration of engineers and the Department for Tutoring and Training, which manifested itself in industrial projects and in the foundation of a Department for Education Technology (Bildungstechnik) at the IPK-Berlin. The task of this new scientific field is the development of teaching and learning procedures, and knowledge and communication systems, while applying know-how and methods by information technology.

Projects concerning tutoring and training extend into larger, contract-related tasks, which focus on the detection of the need for further education, the establishing of adequate courses, and job-specific training courses. Projects such as these offer support particularly for small and medium-sized enterprises during their introductory phase to innovative technologies. This support comprises operating instructions, computer-aided user support, and system-specific orientation courses. Within the framework of measures for further education numerous courses and seminars were organized.

One of the main targets of the performance of transfer is to make new technologies available for practical applications. In trying to achieve this aim, R&D activities are designed in an interdisciplinary way, combining the aspects of various technological disciplines with economic and sociological viewpoints. This is the reason for pursuing the technology transfer in different variations. Another angle of achieving this interdisciplinarity is the purposive foundation of firms and the collaboration in establishing new research institutes. Thirty institutions and firms founded directly by the assistance of the director or by former academic staff bear witness to this practice.

The high level of education of Technische Universität graduates in production-technological subjects was a motivation for using this high potential of knowledge in the automobile industry for the solution of automation tasks. On the director's initiative, renowned firms such as BMW, Mercedes-Benz, Siemens, and Volkswagen founded the INPRO (Innovation Society for Advanced Production Systems in the Automobile Industry) to carry out joint development tasks in the precompetitive phase.

After a short period of time, the INPRO was in a position to supply the automobile industry with useful results concerning important questions. Some major projects were intelligent sensor systems for handling pattern recognition and contour tracking and expert systems for the diagnosis of engine conditions.

An additional foundation united the numerous activities in Berlin, which deal with scientific-technological information processing activities that are indispensable for the automobile industry. The foundation of the software house VW-GEDAS opened the possibility of covering the spectrum of customer-oriented problem analysis, comprising the concept, realization, and maintenance of software systems as well as the tutoring and training sector.

In context with the projects research institutes were founded on an international level. They are comparable with technology centers:

- MEPPO (scientific-technological collaboration with the Republic of Indonesia in the building of an institute for production technology)
- German-Irish initiative, funded by the German-Irish Programme for Collaboration in Science and Technology

Technological transfer of know-how is carried out in the following projects:

- CIM-TT (computer integrated manufacturing, technology transfer)
- FRP-TT (fiber-reinforced plastics, technology transfer)
- WOP center (workshop-oriented programming system)

A specific qualification program introduces academics holding degrees in nontechnological subjects to the science of labor. Graduates of this program have also founded firms, working in the fields of technology design, organizational development, and qualification management.

The Production Technological Colloquium (PTK) is a conference that takes place every 3 years. Ever since its launch in 1979 this scientific conference has proved to be a special form of performance in the transfer of know-how. Numerous representatives from various branches of industry take part in this event on a regular basis. The PTK is known as a form of further education concerning the discussion of the "factory of the future."

Outlook

The future of manufacturing technology in Germany, in Berlin, and at the Production Technology Center will be determined by two facts:

- The European Single Market 1993
- The integration of the new federal Laender (states) into the economy

The European Single Market will soon be the largest in the world. The traditional markets of companies and enterprises will shift and competitiveness is likely to be increased. The customers' demands will also grow and thus their influence on the producers of investment and consumer goods.

A reorientation of company strategies must take place in investment, quality, price, and delivery time of products. Internally the factory has to be reorganized. It will be determined by information technology and the development of new materials. This implies new management strategies which are open to new approaches and interdisciplinary methods, as environmental problems and the motivation for a high-quality performance of the staff will be at the center of discussion.

Research Projects and Graphical Charts

This section describes the organizational structure and research efforts of the Berlin Production Technology Center.

Figures 6.4 through 6.15 graphically describe the scope, size, and composition of the institute, its research, and its personnel. Some of the relevant departments of the Production Technology Center are described below.

Robot systems technology and control systems

- Mathematical modeling of manufacturing processes
- Integration of mathematical models in expert systems
- Dynamic behavior of production components
- Optimal motion planning for industrial robot systems
- Motion planning of cooperating robot systems
- Hybrid position and force control of robots and cooperating robot systems
- Multisensor-guided process control systems
- Knowledge-based tools for development of task-optimized robot controls
- Advanced robot control structures

m DM

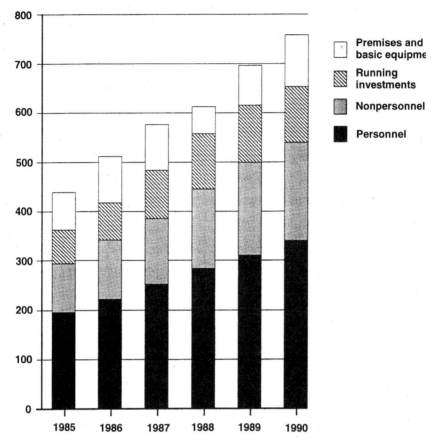

Figure 6.4 Decomposition of total expenses, 1985–1990. *Note:* This figure refers to the Fraunhofer Society in general (not solely to the IPK-Berlin).

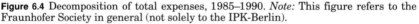

- Communication functions of robot control systems in open CIM system structures
- Controls and programming systems for industrially applied robots
- Off-line programming systems for robots
- Simulation systems for robotized manufacturing cells
- Automatic calibration of industrial robots
- Concepts for lightweight robot design
- Robot systems for space and offshore applications
- Flexible automation of press lines

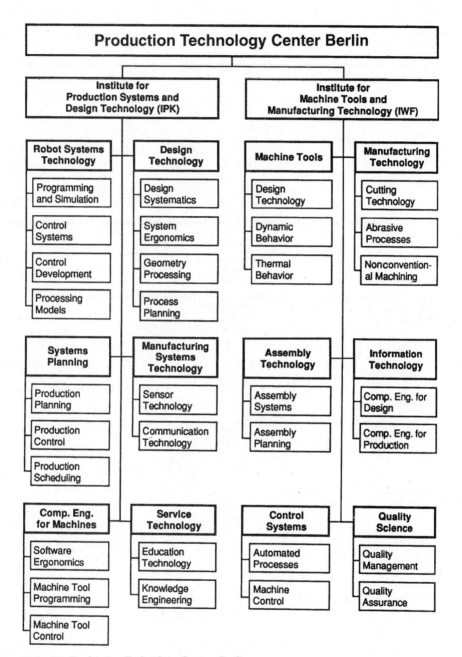

Figure 6.5 Production Technology Center, Berlin.

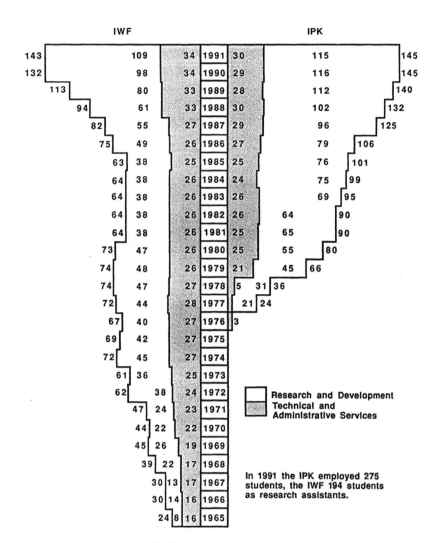

Figure 6.6 Growth of IWF and IPK.

Design technology and information technology

- Fundamental developments for two- and three-dimensional part geometry processing
- Coupling of existing CAD systems with modules for geometry processing, calculation, and technological planning
- Adaptations of existing CAD systems for the expansion of application modules

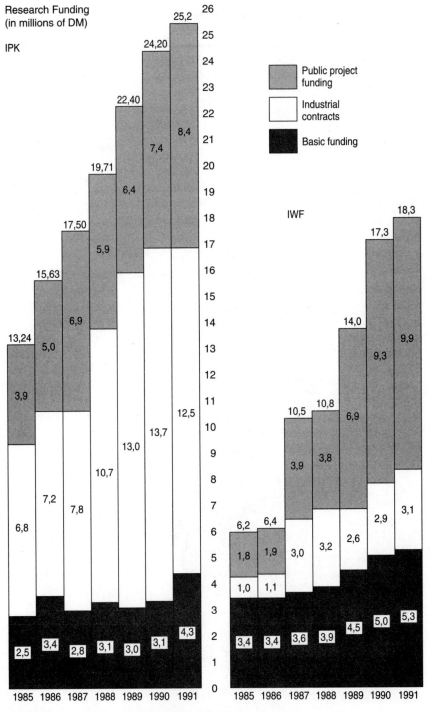

Figure 6.7 Research funding (in millions of DM).

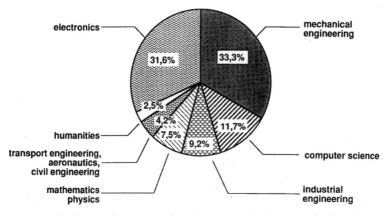

Figure 6.8 Professional training of employees at the Institute for Production Systems and Design Technology.

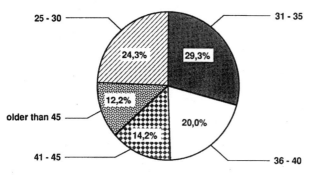

Figure 6.9 Age structure of researchers at the IPK (1991).

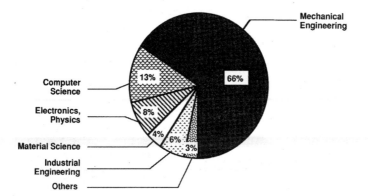

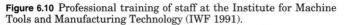

Figure 6.10 Professional training of staff at the Institute for Machine Tools and Manufacturing Technology (IWF 1991).

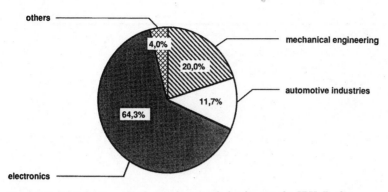

Figure 6.11 Distribution of industrial research funding at the IPK, Berlin.

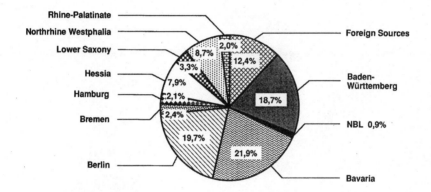

Figure 6.12 Distribution of industrial research funding in the Federal Republic of Germany (IPK), 1991.

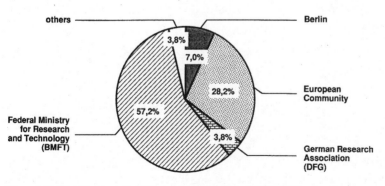

Figure 6.13 Distribution of public research funding (IPK), 1991.

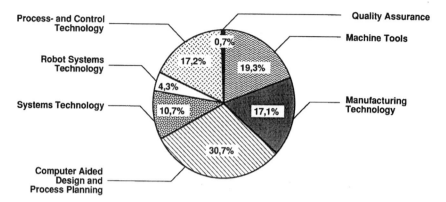

Figure 6.14 Doctoral theses according to subjects (IWF/IPK), 1965–1991.

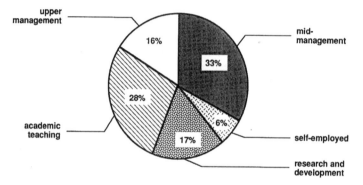

Figure 6.15 Fields of profession of former doctor engineers, 1991.

- Pattern recognition and automated drawing conversion
- Hardware-oriented CAD system architectures
- Man-machine communication for CAD systems
- Parallel processing in CAD systems
- CAD reference models
- Lead time reduction
- Simultaneous engineering
- Off-line programming for planning processes
- Computer-aided technological planning
- Analysis of industrial design and production procedures for the development of CAD-oriented target concepts

- Evaluation of CAD systems (market analysis, selection cataloging, and benchmark techniques)
- Introduction of CAD systems (training, planning, supervision of pilot phases)
- Knowledge engineering in design and production engineering

Systems planning

- Computer simulation for design and optimization of production systems
- Integrated factory design
- Planning of flexible automated manufacturing systems
- Development of information and material flow systems adapted to specific tasks
- Methods to design CIM projects
- Development of CIM architectures
- Part, tool, and capacity scheduling
- Task-related design of robot systems
- Production control, integrated order management
- Competence-oriented shop-floor control systems
- Economic criteria for design and control of automated production structures
- Design of advanced production concepts
- Knowledge-based rule systems for production planning and control
- Systematic product and process innovation
- Qualification and technology for advanced factories

Manufacturing systems technology

- Multisensor systems for process control and quality monitoring
- Image-analyzing systems for testing surfaces
- Sensor systems for object recognition in robotics
- Grippers and integrated sensor systems
- Texture analysis methods for inspection tasks
- Pattern-recognition procedures for sensor-driven tasks
- Design of dedicated, high-performance hardware for image processing

- CIM modeling and implementation strategies
- Standard-based communication technology in open distributed environments
- Pilot applications of CIM infrastructures and components
- Integrated design of distributed shop-floor control systems
- Structured design techniques for PLC programming
- Knowledge-based systems for the support of design
- Machine learning
- Knowledge-based tutoring and training, CAL
- Qualification and branch analysis
- Company-related training programs
- Methods, media, and seminars in support of further qualification programs within the company
- User guidance and tutoring for customers
- Management consultancy

Machine tools
- Computer-aided conception of machine tools
- Knowledge-based design of machine tools
- Clamping of rotation-oriented workpieces
- Shape errors due to clamping forces in turning
- Force sensors for power-operated three-jaw chucks
- Safety at cutting machine tools
- High-speed spindle lubrication
- Process control at cutting machine tools
- Static and dynamic behavior optimization of spindle bearing systems
- Dynamic behavior simulation of cutting machine tools
- Application of new materials in machine tool spindles
- Compensation of spindle displacement caused by thermal effects
- Heat transfer within machine tools
- Deep drawing by use of a servo-hydraulic apparatus

Manufacturing technology
- Machining of ceramics and semiconductor materials
- Machining of fiber-reinforced plastics

- Machining of ferrous and nonferrous metals and high-strength nickel-based alloys
- Polycrystalline cutting tool materials
- Optimization and application of coated cutting tools
- Grinding wheel properties
- Five-axis milling
- Internal thread production
- High-precision machining processes
- Technology of CO_2 and solid-state laser cutting
- Cutting fluids in material-removal processes
- Measurement techniques and sensors in machining
- Thermal image processing
- Modeling and computer-aided simulation of machining processes
- Demonstration and technology transfer center for fiber-reinforced plastics
- Water-jet cutting
- Electric discharge machining

Assembly technology
- Design for ease of assembly
- Computer-aided assembly planning
- Simulation of assembly processes
- Group technology in assembly
- Realization of prototypes for flexible assembly systems
- Test of components for assembly
- Sensor-guided assembly processes
- Knowledge-based diagnosis in assembly processes
- Control of assembly processes
- Advanced robot systems
- Orbital assembly systems
- Market analysis of the development of assembly technology
- Qualification and management

Quality science
- Three-coordinate measuring center for quality control of production

- Flexible metrology cell for NC manufacturing
- Quality assurance at design level through quality function deployment (QFD)
- Quality data preparation for CAD applications
- Evaluation of quality assurance systems
- Auditing techniques for quality assurance systems
- Quality techniques for management
- Quality control for the realization of just-in-time production
- Quality management as a contribution to work organization
- Information system for management concerning costs during manufacturing

Summary

This chapter describes the history and operation of the Berlin Production Technology Center. By the cooperation of the Institute for Machine Tools and Manufacturing Technology of the Technical University of Berlin and the Fraunhofer Institute of Production Systems and Design Technology, it represents a symbiosis of basic and applied research in factory automation. The chapter includes a description of the basic concept of the Fraunhofer Society, a nonprofit organization of 37 institutes focusing on applied research in the fields of natural science and technology. It also describes a number of research projects realized at the Berlin Production Technology Center during recent years.

Small and Medium-Sized Industries in R.O.C.: A Model Policy for Continued Growth

Ching Wen Li

Associate Professor
National Taipei Institute of Technology
Taipei, R.O.C.

A Brief History

The Republic of China (R.O.C.) is a trade and manufacturing oriented country with great potential for development. On tracing its economic development since 1952, we can see that the R.O.C. has undergone tremendous economic reform. Through the joint efforts of the government and its people in implementing a national policy for small and medium business, the R.O.C. has implemented many development programs and has taken the necessary measures to bring about Taiwan's strong economic growth. The R.O.C. is now ranked as the sixteenth largest trading country in the world.

These achievements have impressed many countries in the world, and therefore the R.O.C. can be used by other similar countries as a role model for economic development.

The small and medium-sized enterprises in the R.O.C. are closely intertwined with the development and enforcement of educational and economic measures adopted by the government.

The successful implementation of a "Land-to-the-Tiller" program provided the momentum to improve agricultural productivity and turned an underemployed labor force in the rural areas into worker resources of small and medium-sized enterprises, thus laying a sound foundation for their development.

Successive economic development plans formulated and implemented by the government have served to build on each other and have assured the success of rapid economic growth. The implementation of a 9-year compulsory education program for all citizens has made possible the building up of a reservoir of labor for small and medium-sized enterprises; the industriousness of the people coupled with effective assistance rendered by the government have helped spur the continuous growth and expansion of the burgeoning small and medium enterprises. Moreover, the strong social order in the R.O.C. has provided an excellent development environment for such enterprises.

Background

Taiwan, surrounded by water, has a subtropical climate which favors agriculture. Mineral resources are scarce, thus providing for limited economic development. The island is 36,000 square kilometers in area with a maximum north-south length of 400 kilometers and an east-west dimension of 200 kilometers. Most manufacturing enterprises were traditionally small and midsize, with products from the enterprises geared primarily toward the domestic market. This was historically due to the lack of investment capital, techniques, and raw materials.

The government of the R.O.C. began to take measures to increase industrial production in 1964. In order to meet the strong demand from international markets and with the aid of both domestic and foreign trade partners, enterprises began to change the management methods of businesses and also improved the quality of products. Thus the export business of the Republic of China was on its way.

The oil crises in the 1970s provided the first challenge to small and medium-sized enterprises. However, local businesspeople offset the impact by training professionals to improve businesses, and improved the quality of products. The enterprises began to utilize computers and peripherals during this time. They focused on the local market, establishing a positive image for indigenous products. These enterprises still needed to improve management and change production structures because of the worldwide recession and strong competition from other countries which had policies of internationalization and liberalization.

Definition of Small and
Medium-Sized Enterprises

An enterprise is defined as a small or medium-sized enterprise if it meets one of the following criteria:

1. Manufacturing or construction industry with invested capital less than $1.6 million and total assets less than $4.8 million
2. Mining industry with invested capital less than $1.6 million
3. Any commercial or transportation or other service industry with previous annual sales revenue less than $1.6 million
4. Other industries with annual sales revenues less than $1.6 million

Moreover, if an enterprise grows to a size greater than the above-mentioned standards with the assistance of government, it is still considered as a small or medium-sized enterprise for 2 years; if it grows to a size greater than the standards as a result of merger through government assistance, it is still regarded as a small or medium-sized enterprise for 3 years.

It can be seen from Fig. 7.1 that small and medium-sized enterprises with invested capital less than $40,000 account for 35.7 percent of the total number of small and medium-sized enterprises; those with an invested capital between $40,000 and $200,000 account for 42.8 percent of these enterprises, while only 21.3 percent of these enterprises have an invested capital of over $200,000.

Figure 7.2 shows that over two-thirds of small and medium-sized enterprises employ less than 20 people while only 5.4 percent of these enterprises employ over 100 people. More than 98 percent of the total number of enterprises (i.e., 700,000) in the R.O.C. are small and

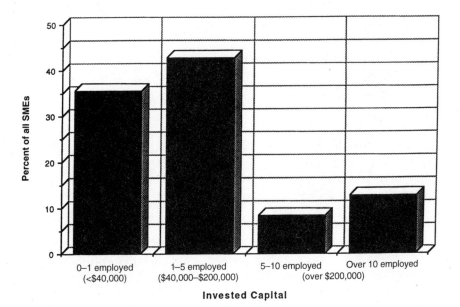

Figure 7.1 Invested capital of small and medium-sized enterprises (SMEs).

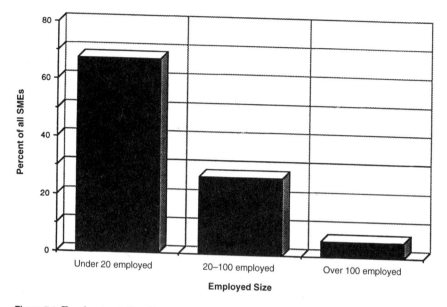

Figure 7.2 Employment distribution of SMEs.

medium-sized enterprises; the manufacturing industry accounts for about 17 percent of the total, the service industry 16 percent, and commerce 61 percent. The amounts of capital invested range from NT$1 million to NT$5 million. The average number of employees of small and medium-sized enterprises is less than 20.

The Role of Small and Medium-Sized Enterprises in the R.O.C.

There are more than 700,000 small and medium-sized enterprises in Taiwan; this accounts for more than 98 percent of the total number of enterprises in the R.O.C. These enterprises also represent 65 percent of the total export volume, 55 percent of the GNP, and 70 percent of the total employed population of the R.O.C. It can therefore be seen that small and medium enterprises continue to be the major force in the economic development of the R.O.C.

Of the more than 700,000 small and medium-sized enterprises, the manufacturing industry accounts for about 17 percent of the total, the service industry 16 percent, and commerce 61 percent (Fig. 7.3). It should also be noted, however, that many commerce and trading industries do business with manufacturing and manufacturing related products.

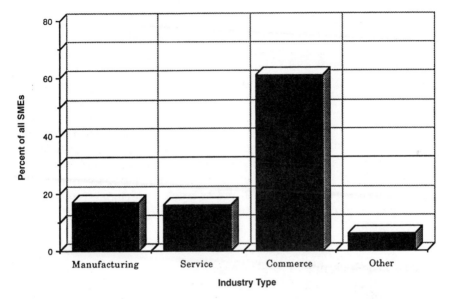

Figure 7.3 Demographic profile of SMEs.

The Characteristics of Small and Medium-Sized Enterprises

Small and medium-sized enterprises in the Republic of China can typically be characterized as follows:

1. They are family-managed and family-operated.
2. Owners of enterprises are well educated and have working experience.
3. Most of the newly founded enterprises are run by an aggressive new generation.

Problems Faced with Small and Medium-Sized Enterprises

Since most small and medium-sized enterprises are family-run, they are strongly influenced by the social structure of the family and society; this has both advantages and disadvantages.

Small and medium-sized enterprises often lack the equipment and expertise to upgrade technical levels, thus lowering productivity. This is typically due to limitations of capital. Private loans entail high interest rates and bank loans are not easy to obtain. In addition, these enterprises are limited by the lack of sophisticated marketing capability and availability. These factors, coupled with the fact that small and medium-sized enterprises also have to face strong competition from other countries, limit their continued development and growth.

The economic situation of these enterprises has also been made more difficult with increasing international trade protectionism and appreciation of the New Taiwan dollar in recent years. Lacking the skills of professional management operations, these small and medium-sized enterprises are burdened with a heavy pressure. Therefore, the government has had to render proper assistance and guidance, helping them break barriers and create a competitive edge for the future.

The R.O.C. Government Assistance Programs for Small and Medium-Sized Enterprises

Assistance policies

Economic policy of the R.O.C. is based on the philosophy of its founding father, Dr. Sun Yat-sen, which calls for an equitable distribution of wealth and opportunities. The government of the R.O.C. has formulated a systematic and ongoing policy that provides small and medium-sized enterprises with many different types of assistance. The assistance and services provided are in the three areas of technology, management, and financing.

The objectives that government expects to achieve are described as follows:

1. To improve the business environment
2. To rationalize business management
3. To enhance the availability of capital specifically for the development of small and medium-sized enterprises
4. To encourage mergers in order to enlarge business operation, or to promote mutual cooperation in order to enhance competitiveness
5. To encourage private and large enterprises to assist small and medium-sized enterprises in establishing central and satellite factory systems

The Role of Medium and Small Business Administration (MSBA)

The R.O.C. government began to offer small and medium-sized enterprises different forms of assistance in 1964. After the worldwide recession resulting from the oil crisis, with an aim to further promote the development of small and medium-sized enterprises, the Ministry of Economic Affairs established the Medium and Small Business Administration in 1981. This government agency offers the following assistance:

1. Financial assistance

2. Management assistance

3. Technology assistance

4. Financial and accounting assistance

5. Marketing assistance

6. Computerization assistance

7. Assistance in coping with appreciation of the New Taiwan dollar

The objective of these initiatives was to ensure smooth circulation of capital, strengthening the financial structure, introducing new technology and equipment, and promoting modernization of business management. Figure 7.4 illustrates the assistance systems of MSBA.

Financial assistance

Loan extension, credit guarantee, and financial review are provided by this subsystem. In addition to using general banks such as the Bank of Taiwan, the Bank of Transportation, the Cooperative Bank, and other general commercial banks, the MSBA utilizes the Medium Business Bank of Taiwan to take charge of the loan services. Small and medium-sized enterprises usually find it difficult to provide the collateral when they wish to obtain loans from banks. Therefore, the Small Business Credit Guarantee Fund was formed by the government with the assistance of bank donations to provide the necessary collateral in helping such enterprises obtain required loans.

Services provided by the Small Business Integrated Center include assistance in the application of capital to establish financial and accounting systems, and in the review of loan proposals for those small and medium-sized enterprises that are unable to obtain loans, with an eye to helping them improve. Financial assistance avenues

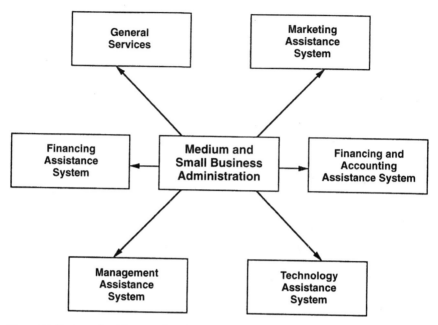

Figure 7.4 System of guidance and assistance.

that are open to small and medium-sized enterprises are summarized in Fig. 7.5.

Management assistance

Management assistance generally involves several different services. For example, a management consulting company may be entrusted to conduct research and analysis at no cost to the client, to help small and medium-sized enterprises improve their competitive edge. Retired experts both at home and abroad may be employed to utilize their broad knowledge and experience to objectively supervise improvement of production technology and management skills. This valuable service helps to accelerate the process of modernization of the small and medium-sized enterprises.

The China Productivity Center focuses on technology transfer and management assistance to these small and medium-sized industries. Resources of universities and colleges are also utilized in providing this type of assistance. The Industrial Technology Research Institute (ITRI) is a center for applied research for different types of small and medium-sized industry. The types of research projects conducted are based directly on the needs of local industry. This research is primar-

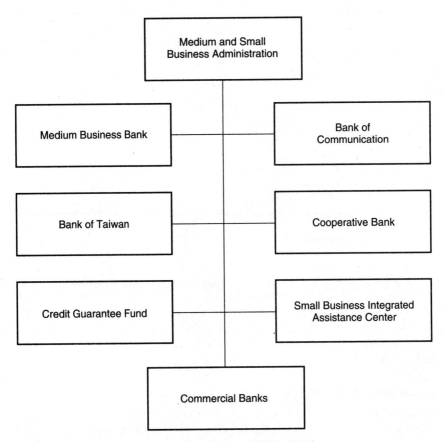

Figure 7.5 Financing assistance system. (*Source: MSBA, 1989.*)

ily funded by the government at no cost to the client. If appropriate, research findings are transferred to small and medium-sized enterprises for immediate commercial applications. These initiatives are summarized in Fig. 7.6.

Technology assistance

Figure 7.7 details the different aspects of technology assistance. In the area of production management and technological assistance, the administration utilizes the consultant service facilities, research equipment, and expertise of related organizations affiliated with the production assistance system to help improve production techniques, raise productivity, and develop new products so as to strengthen the competitiveness of small and medium-sized enterprises.

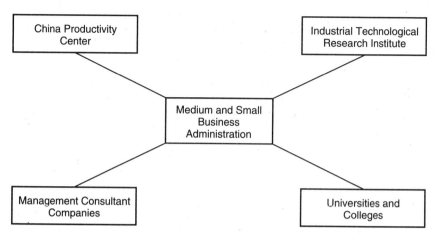

Figure 7.6 Management assistance system. (*Source: MSBA, 1989.*)

Small and medium-sized enterprises are usually deficient on a managerial as well as on a technical level, so that seminars and training programs are very important to them. These training courses cover such areas as government policies, financing regulations and laws, management, and production technology and have successfully cultivated many talented people over the past few years.

Accounting assistance (Fig. 7.8)

Many small and medium-sized enterprises do not have the training and background necessary for implementing and managing efficient accounting systems. The Medium and Small Business Administration unites into one body educational institutions and banking agencies to schedule seminars for educating and assisting in these areas. In addition, it formally requests the Accountants Association to appoint accountants with proven experience in directing medium and small enterprises in establishing an improved accounting system.

Marketing assistance (Fig. 7.9)

To counter the blow brought by the sharp appreciation of the NT dollar against the U.S. dollar, MSBA explains foreign exchange and its operations to entrepreneurs. In addition, assistance is provided to explore European markets with the help of the China External Trade Development Council (CETDC), the Board of Foreign Trade, and all the related monetary facilities. A sustained economic growth and employment growth through optimal exploitation of both domestic and overseas markets is the goal of the MSBA marketing assistance system.

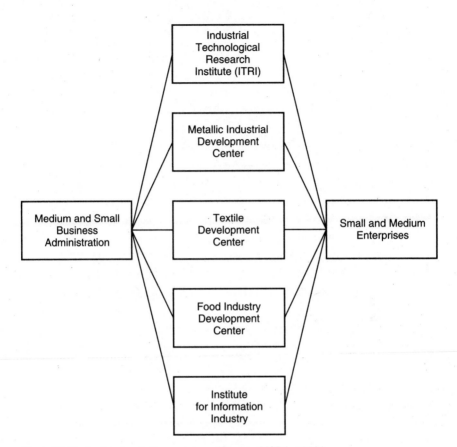

Figure 7.7 Technology assistance system. (*Source: MSBA, 1989.*)

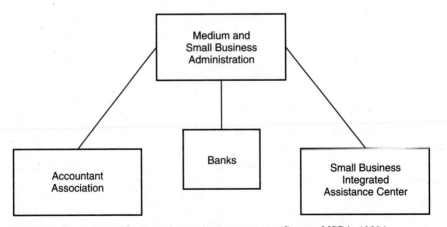

Figure 7.8 Financing and accounting assistance system. (*Source: MSBA, 1989.*)

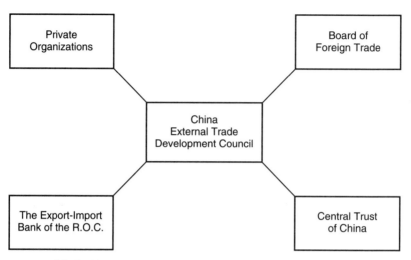

Figure 7.9 Marketing assistance system. (*Source: MSBA, 1989.*)

Computerization assistance

The computer is an indispensable management tool in modern business. Its major functions are to store, count, and process information quickly and accurately so as to firmly grasp advantageous timing and promote scientific management and systemization. With a view toward effectively promoting the computerization of enterprises, the assistance agency offers necessary services through the cooperation and support of private computer firms.

Assistance in coping with appreciation of the New Taiwan dollar

Since 1986, when the large-scale appreciation of the New Taiwan dollar began, the administration, hoping to help small and medium-sized enterprises cope with the pressure caused by the appreciation, has actively assisted them in restructuring in order to enhance competitiveness. The administration also helps them reduce loss due to this appreciation through the buying and selling of foreign exchange and diversification of international markets in coordination with concerned agencies.

In order to stimulate the continuous growth of domestic industrial and commercial business and raise investment willingness, the government has drawn up regulations governing tax reduction or exemption which can apply to small and medium-sized enterprises. The Medium and Small Business Administration of the Ministry of

Economic Affairs is responsible for the implementation of the above-mentioned assistance measures. The major functions of the administration include strengthening relations with small and medium-sized enterprises, as well as solving problems for them, and offering assistance in management, technology, and finance.

According to Article 2 of the organizational statutes of the administration, the administration has the following functions: to draw up plans or regulations related to the development of small and medium-sized enterprises; and to conduct surveys, research, and assistance on technical improvement, training programs, management, and financial affairs. Another priority is to promote international cooperation between small and medium-sized enterprises and foreign companies.

Besides the three departments affiliated within the administration, regional service centers have been set up in Hsinchu, Taichung, Tainan, Kaohsiung, and Ilan. They aim to strengthen local links with small and medium-sized enterprises, facilitate services and dissemination of information, help them restructure and raise productivity, upgrade products, and adjust management tactics, thus creating new horizons for these enterprises.

Union Service Center

In order to serve small and medium-sized enterprises in a comprehensive manner, a union service center was founded in June 1988. Its regional service centers are in Hsinchu, Taichung, Tainan, Kaohsiung, and Ilan. A map of the location of each center on the island is shown in Fig. 7.10. There is ongoing communication between each regional service center and its affiliated small and medium-sized enterprises, providing not only technical assistance but also the latest information on international events, enabling entrepreneurs to adjust their management policies and improve their global competitiveness.

The Functions of Regional Service Centers

1. To contact and communicate with small and medium-sized enterprises to realize their problems and needs.

2. To announce guidance measures offered by governments and to provide the small and medium-sized enterprises with service information.

3. To recommend qualified agencies to help the local enterprises.

4. To provide diagnostic information to solve the problems encountered by local small and medium-sized enterprises.

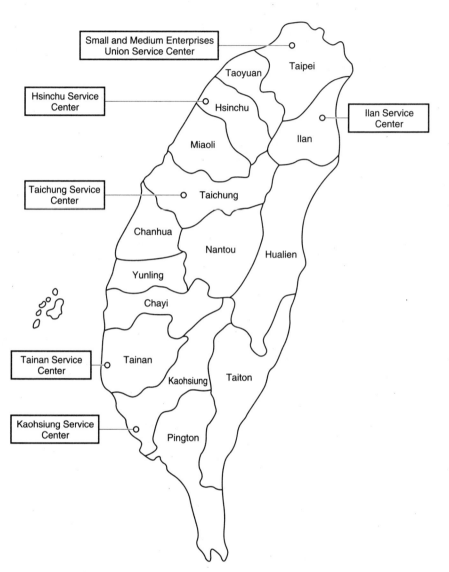

Figure 7.10 Medium and Small Business Administration regional service centers. (*Source: MSBA, 1989.*)

5. To hire an expert or a consultant to help the small and medium-sized enterprises to solve their problems.

6. To offer the small and medium-sized enterprises workshops and academic, technical, and observational training.

Each regional service center is an outreach-type office with three to five employees. These regional centers maintain close contact with

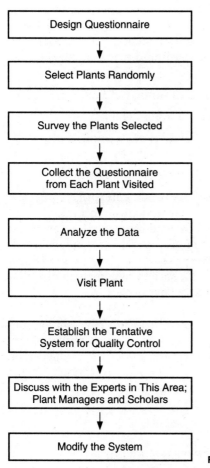

Figure 7.11 System for quality control.

local industry and are the "eyes and ears" of the union service center. Many more regional service centers are in the planning stage.

Case study

During the last few years, a concerted effort has been made to establish quality control systems in small and medium-sized enterprises. The basic steps taken to establish the system for quality control are described in Fig. 7.11.

Conclusion

By the year 2000, the R.O.C. is projected to attain developed nation status with an estimated per capita annual income projected at

$15,000. Accordingly, the continued development of small and medium-sized enterprises is needed, since these enterprises are the backbone of the R.O.C.'s industry. In order to meet future needs, the administration will continue to assist small and medium-sized enterprises in creating better opportunities in the following manner:

1. Providing the enterprises with an environment of fair competition
2. Assisting the enterprises with modern management
3. Promoting automated production techniques, raising energy efficiency, and upgrading products
4. Assisting the enterprises to expand international markets

We strongly believe that small and medium-sized enterprises, with the assistance of the government and agencies and through mutual cooperation between these businesses, will become stronger than ever and continue to be a backbone of society. In line with the principle of a balanced development between large enterprises and small and medium-sized enterprises, we will stride toward a society of equitable distribution of wealth using the policies formulated by the MSBA.

Acknowledgment. The help and guidance of Ru-Cing Hsu, senior specialist and section chief, Medium and Small Business Administration, Ministry of Economic Affairs, R.O.C., is gratefully acknowledged. The author would also like to thank J. T. Chang, president, National Taipei Institute of Technology, for his continued support.

References

Substantial material for this chapter was adopted from the following publications from the Medium and Small Business Administration, Ministry of Economic Affairs, R.O.C.:

1. Ministry of Economic Affairs, *Measures to Develop and Assist Small and Medium Enterprises,* Medium and Small Business Administration, Ministry of Economic Affairs, Republic of China, Taipei, 1989.
2. Ministry of Economic Affairs, *Medium and Small Business Administration—Ministry of Economic Affairs and Its Objectives,* Medium and Small Business Administration, Ministry of Economic Affairs, Republic of China, Taipei, 1989.
3. Ministry of Economic Affairs, *Growth and Leaping Upward—The Development of Small and Medium Enterprises in the Republic of China,* Medium and Small Business Administration, Ministry of Economic Affairs, Republic of China, Taipei, January 1989.
4. Ministry of Economic Affairs, *Growth and Surging Upward—The Development of Small and Medium Enterprises in the Republic of China,* Medium and Small Business Administration, Ministry of Economic Affairs, Republic of China, Taipei, June 1989.

8

CETIM: A Shared Manufacturing Model in France

Pierre Padilla

Centre Technique des Industries Mecaniques
Senlis, France

The French Manufacturing Industry

French manufacturing industries embody a wide range of activities and a great variety of different products, producing capital goods, equipment for every kind of industry, components, etc. The most important activities include the manufacture of

- Machine tools
- Refrigerating and thermal equipment
- Engines, compressors, and turbines
- Equipment for food processing, chemical, and plastics industries
- Textile equipment
- Equipment for the papermaking industry
- Equipment for construction, iron and steel, casting, and mining industries
- Material handling equipment
- Agricultural machinery

They also produce components and small equipment, such as bolts, springs, hardware and small metal articles, machinery tools and gears, valves, fittings, hydraulic and pneumatic transmissions, pumps, bearings, measuring, weighing, and regulation equipment, and medicosurgical equipment.

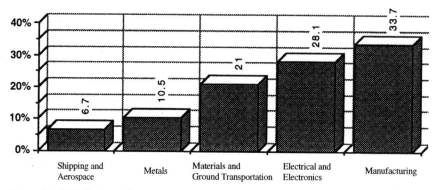

Figure 8.1 Distribution of wage earners.

Figure 8.1 provides an overview of the complexity and diversity of the mechanical industry in France and shows that it is a vital branch of the industrial economy, with an approximate 323 billion francs ($65.5 billion) turnover. This represents approximately 12 percent of French industry turnover and places France sixth in the world in terms of production. Of this production, goods for a value of 143 billion francs ($29 billion) are exported, which helps make France the fifth largest exporter in the world. Figure 8.2 shows the primary export markets of France. Figure 8.3 shows France's share of overall EEC production.

The manufacturing industry sector is composed of over 7000 firms, which have approximately 550,000 employees. A classification of companies according to the number of employees is given in Table 8.1. It can be seen that over 80 percent of French manufacturing industry is

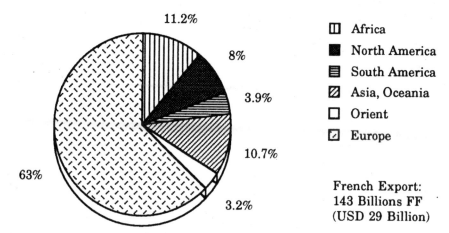

Figure 8.2 French export partners.

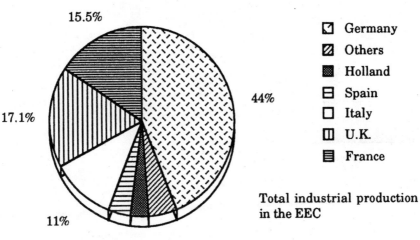

Figure 8.3 French production in the EEC.

TABLE 8.1 Classification of Companies

No. of employees in the company	No. of companies, %	No. of employees, %	Turnover, %
20–99	83.5	41.7	34.6
100–499	13.7	32.5	31.7
Over 500	2.8	25.8	33.7
Total	100.0	100.0	100.0

TABLE 8.2 Comparison of Employee Category

Employee category	1975	1989
Engineers and managers	8.6	11.3
Technicians	14.7	16.9
Qualified workers	42.2	47.4
Nonqualified workers	34.5	24.4
Total, %	100.0	100.0

comprised of companies with less than 99 employees. These companies account for over 40 percent of those employed in manufacturing and account for over a third of total turnover. The technical level of the employees in this sector has also increased over the years, following the technical advances in the area, as shown in Table 8.2.

The economic and industrial activity of the manufacturing sector is distributed throughout the country, with a higher concentration in the region around Paris (Ile de France) and the Rhône-Alps region.

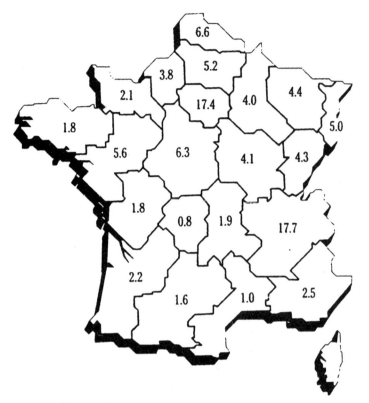

Figure 8.4 Geographical dispersion of manufacturing industries.

The map (Fig. 8.4) shows the geographical dispersion of the manufacturing industries.

As we can see from Table 8.1, more than 80 percent of the companies in the manufacturing sector have fewer than 100 employees and more than 90 percent of the companies have fewer than 500 employees. Seventy-five percent of the employees are concentrated in these companies as well as more than 65 percent of the total turnover, which shows us the importance of the small and midsize enterprises (SMEs).

It is important to notice that in other developed countries like Germany and the United Kingdom, and in general in the European Community, the percentage of SMEs and their economic importance are similar.

Definition of SMEs

Because of the importance of SMEs, we provide the different parameters currently used for defining an SME. This definition can be given basically by quantitative or qualitative parameters:

Quantitative. The basic parameters are the number of employees and the turnover of the enterprise. A company is considered an SME if it has fewer than 500 employees and a turnover of less than 270 million francs (these parameters are suggested in the European contracts for the eligibility of an SME).

Qualitative. Three parameters define an SME:

1. The management style: The manager or chief executive officer personally assumes and directs all the economic, financial, technical, social, and moral responsibilities, whichever their legal form is.

2. Property and independence: An SME is a company held and managed by an independent proprietor.

3. The Small Business Act defines an SME based on market share as a company owned and managed in an independent manner that does not monopolize its activity sector.

SMEs as defined above can include companies with very different characteristics. It is obvious that a company with 500 employees is structured and managed in a very different way than a company with 20 employees, and there are significant differences in their functions and purposes (final products vs. subcontractor), the technical level and quality of products, their economic influence, etc.

It is evident that, independent of the size, structure, or purpose, every company has a strong necessity for information in order to survive and grow in an environment of changing technology and strong competition, not only nationally, but also internationally. With adequate technological and economic information, a company can assure or increase the quality and competitiveness of their products, proceedings, and services in order to keep or increase their market share. For example, the larger companies demand increasingly high quality levels in order to extend quality certifications to their subcontractors.

Depending on the available information, a company can decide to diversify their activities and, for example, not only be a subcontractor but also produce final products or even have a radical change of activities.

The type of information an SME needs includes:

- Practical, concise, and fast information about suppliers of products and services, regulations, standards and specifications, techniques, etc.

- Information and inquiries about the technology in the company's domain, development of new technologies, means of production, control, etc.

- Reports and reviews analyzing and synthesizing scientific information covering specific subjects.

There are many and different sources of information: general and specialized press, professional associations, technical centers, conferences, meetings and proceedings, exhibitions, suppliers and vendors, etc. Paradoxically, we find many companies faced with problems of lack of information or with an information overflow. This especially happens in the SMEs where the manager or chief of the enterprise, owing to multiple responsibilities, is unable to search for information, has no time to evaluate this information, and/or does not disseminate the useful information in the company. For the solution of specific problems it may be necessary for an enterprise to research and develop a new technological product. This R&D may be carried out either in the enterprise (internal R&D) or outside the enterprise (external R&D).

Internal R&D.   In this case, the company has the human and material resources for carrying out its own R&D. This is normally the case of big companies or of very innovative SMEs.

External R&D.   In this context, the enterprises normally acquire knowledge generated in external companies, such as universities, research centers, and technical centers. This R&D can be conducted externally under contract or utilizing equipment, systems, licenses, or patents developed by these centers.

Because of the costs associated with R&D programs, SMEs normally use the second approach to solve their need for information on technological developments. This need is the rationale behind the wide network of industrial technological centers, based on the concept of shared manufacturing (centres techniques industriels—CTI), that have been created in France. These centers cover a wide range of industrial activities and are located all over the country. The CTI network is composed of:

18 technical centers

39 establishments and laboratories

50 regional delegations, offices, and training centers

The centers have more than 4000 employees with a yearly budget of approximately 2.5 billion francs. Among these centers, the CETIM—Centre Technique des Industries Mecaniques—helps industries in the manufacturing sector solve their technological problems.

CETIM

CETIM was founded in 1965 by the French Association of Mechanical Engineering Industries (FIMTM) as a collective technical research center, under a government act in 1948. Its purpose is to "contribute to the development of research, the improvement in productivity and quality assurance in the manufacturing industries and, in general, to further technological progress in these industries."

CETIM has a decentralized structure, with establishments located in three strategic cities, Senlis, Nantes, and Saint-Etienne, and 16 regional delegations with a staff of 658 employees. The distribution of CETIM's employees is shown in Table 8.3.

There is also a software marketing department, called PROGE-TIM, located in Roissy and responsible for the marketing and diffusion of the CETIM software.

CETIM had a budget in 1991 of 390 million francs ($79 million). The resources for this budget are as follows:

- 68.1 percent: special levies
- 26.0 percent: services and products
- 5.9 percent: public contracts and miscellaneous

This budget was allocated for the following activities:

- 37.8 percent: collective research
- 31.9 percent: direct assistance
- 4.9 percent: literature and publications
- 6.2 percent: professional training
- 6.1 percent: standardization
- 13.1 percent: regional activity, conferences, and exhibitions

TABLE 8.3   Distribution of Employees in CETIM

Location	Engineers	Technicians	Management	Workers	Total
General management	6	—	—	2	8
Central services	58	18	61	1	138
Establishment Senlis	156	104	43	21	324
Establishment Saint-Etienne	41	37	22	2	102
Establishment Nantes	28	39	14	5	86
Total	289	198	140	31	658

Organizational structure

Since CETIM was created by the FIMTM and its goal is to aid the manufacturing industries, its organizational structure includes representatives of industrial associations and chambers, heads of enterprises, which form the board of trustees, and representatives of government. The board of trustees nominates a general director. A technical committee has the function of advising the general director in technical and scientific matters. The technical commissions are organs that establish the communication between the mechanical professional sector and CETIM, and are thus involved in the research trends and the diffusion of the results. The general organizational structure of CETIM is shown in Fig. 8.5.

CETIM's mission

CETIM's mission comprises three complementary activities, as shown in Fig. 8.6, which are performed in close contact with the

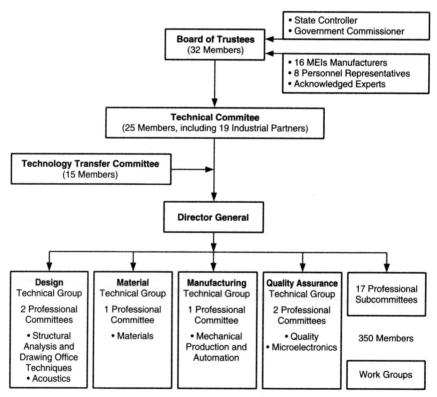

Figure 8.5 Organizational structure—CETIM.

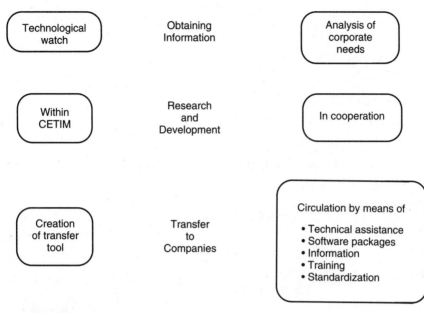

Figure 8.6 CETIM's mission.

entire manufacturing engineering profession. These three activities cover a wide range of sectors in the mechanical industry, among them:

- Design

    Computer-aided design

    Structural analysis

    Choice and performances of materials

- Production

    Organization and methods analysis

    Automation of production

    Knowledge of working methods

    - Cutting of materials, machining
    - Cutting and forming of iron sheets
    - Forging
    - Treatments and coating of metals
    - Working of polymers and composites
    - Assembly methods

- Control and quality

    Measurements

    Nondestructive control

    Industrial acoustics

    Analysis and control of machines

    Quality

- Machines, controls, and components

    Mechanical, hydraulic, and pneumatic transmissions

    Industrial hydraulics

    Fluid sealing

    Microelectronics of products

    Applied thermodynamics

- Rational use of energy

- Protection of the environment, etc.

In order to achieve the three main activities in all these sectors, CETIM has the organizational structure shown in Fig. 8.5 distributed in its three establishments.

The activities of CETIM

Obtain available information. CETIM has two basic functions for accomplishing this task: Keep a constant watch on manufacturing engineering technology all over the world, and compare this information with the requirements of the French industry.

CETIM collects scientific and technical information from a great variety of sources, national as well as international: scientific and technical publications, theses, studies, specialized trade journals, reports of technical standards, conferences, exhibitions, and contacts with research and educational organizations. The gathered information is evaluated, selected, adapted, synthesized, and even translated by the personnel of CETIM.

For collecting and analyzing the requirements of the industry, there are also different channels.

Direct contacts with the companies, through visits from the personnel of the three establishments and the regional delegations

Close relations with the profession, via the trade associations, in order to know the collective requirements

Technical committees and work groups, which constitute organs of direct communication between the industry representatives and

CETIM, and are directly involved in the orientation of its collective research work

Individual requests from companies for training, technical assistance, services, and products

Conferences, seminars, exhibitions

Research and development

The second main activity of CETIM is the research and development of new technologies in the manufacturing field in order to efficiently support the industry with respect to the technological challenge it faces.

At CETIM each year approximately 100 new projects are undertaken, most of them of a shared nature, as they are the result of consultations with the industrial sectors. The major part of the research is carried out in CETIM's laboratories, and many of them are in partnership with other French organizations, such as other members of the CTI network, universities, and of course, industrial partners.

The dialogue and cooperation between industry, universities, and research centers have led to projects that contribute to the application of the most productive technologies.

CETIM is also strongly involved in ongoing European research projects, participating in the following European initiatives:

- Brite
- Sprint
- Comett
- Esprit
- Eureka

CETIM has actually about 20 European research contracts with 90 partners and firms. Some of the ongoing research projects are shown in Table 8.4.

CETIM is also widening its sphere of activity to other continents by pursuing contracts, cooperation agreements, and projects with countries such as Thailand, China, Venezuela, and Mexico.

Technology transfer to industry

The third main activity at CETIM is to transfer the acquired knowledge to the industry. There are different means by which engineering companies can obtain the elements that solve their technical problems:

- Direct assistance

TABLE 8.4   Some Ongoing European Research Projects

Program	Name of project	Main partner	Associated partners
BRITE	Laser welding of thin metal sheet	RTM (Italy)	CETIM Renault (France) GVC (Italy) Liverpool Univ. (GB)
BRITE	Heavy section laser welding	RTM (Italy)	CETIM, ETCA (France) ILT (Germany) CRIF (Belgium) Creusot-Loire Ind. (France) CGE-Sciaky (France)
ESPRIT	MAGIC: Method for Advanced Group Technology Integrated with CAD/CAM	WTCM (Belgium)	CETIM LVD (Belgium) M. Van de Wiele NV (Belgium) CAP SESA Industrie (France) Marcs (Spain) Eigner (Germany)
COMETT	Computer-aided education in composite and naval construction—phase 3	CETIM	INEGI (Portugal) ENSM Nantes (France) Eng. School. San Sebastian (Spain)
COMETT	SEMIRAMIS: Computer-aided education in dimensional metrology	CETIM	Buckinghamshire College (GB) Univ. Polytecnica de Madrid (Spain) Univ. Dortmund (Germany) Univ. Cath. Louvain (Belgium) Univ. Liege (Belgium)
ESPRIT	ANNIE: Application of Neural Networks in Europe	Harwell Laboratory (GB)	CETIM, Alpha S.A. (Greece) British Aerospace PLC (GB) IBP Pietzsch Gmbh. (Germany) Siemens A.G. (Germany) Artificial Intelligence Ltd. (GB)
BRITE	Development of an expert system for tool wear monitoring in milling, drilling, and blanking	CETIM	Brunel Univ. (GB) IAT (Spain) N. Correa (Spain) CT-DEC (France) CTC (Greece) Heriot Watt (GB)
BRITE EURAM	Optimizing structural fiber composites by hybridization	Loughborough University (GB)	CETIM PERA (GB) SINTEE (Norway)
ESPRIT	IPDES: Integrated Product Design System	CETIM	Charmilles Techno (Switzerland) Ecole Central de Lyon (France) IDS, Mecanica de la Pena (France) Tech. Hochschule Darmstadt (Germany) Matra Datavision (France) Gildemeister (Germany) Kade Tech (France) Deltacam Systems (GB) Coretech International (France) Exapt (France)

TABLE 8.4   Some Ongoing European Research Projects *(Continued)*

Program	Name of project	Main partner	Associated partners
BRITE EURAM	Designing methodologies for engineering components	Lucas Engineering (GB)	CETIM Philips (Holland) Univ. Hull (GB)
BRITE EURAM	IDEFIX: Tools and methods for ideal fixturing of mechanical workpieces with modular systems	Techniker (Spain)	CETIM Fatronik (Spain) CRIF (Belgium) FMC (Belgium) Norelem (France)
SPRINT	A vehicle to develop a technology transfer network for mechanical industries	CETIM	AIMME (Spain) BIBA (Germany) CRIF (Belgium) EOLAS (Ireland) PERA (GB) TNO (Holland) Techniker (Spain)
BRITE EURAM	Composite materials for marine structures and components	Cetena (Italy)	CETIM, ENSM (France) Univ. Lisbonne (Portugal) SNIA BPB (Italy) Fincantieri (Italy) Ifremer (France) Bureau Veritas (France)
BRITE EURAM	Quality assurance and reduced leadtime for cutting operations	Stichting voor Produktie Techniek (Holland)	CETIM TNO (Holland) CRIF (Belgium) IVF (Sweden) Aérospatiale (France)

- Training
- Information
- Software packages
- Standardization and certification

Direct assistance.   Many companies confront CETIM with precise and detailed questions in the following manner:

- Using a telephone hot line service (15,000 calls each year)
- Bibliographical researches of all kinds
- Specific studies
- Requests for tests, controls, examinations, and measurements
- Expert surveys, advice

The distribution of assistance requests according to company size can be seen in Fig. 8.7. The SMEs represent 77.5 percent of the direct

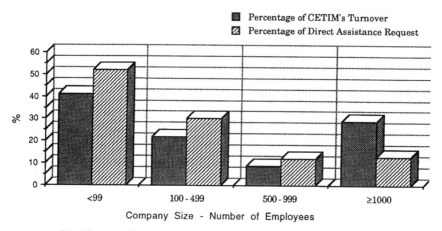

Figure 8.7 Distribution of direct assistance requests according to company size.

assistance requests and 63.4 percent of the turnover. It is important to note the role of small industries in these figures. Requests from industries with more than 1000 employees have also increased significantly in the last years.

Training. The manufacturing industry has a strong need of specialized personnel in up-to-date technologies. The training sessions offered by CETIM are essentially of a practical nature and are held by technical specialists in each area, using all kinds of educational media.

CETIM has a yearly catalog of 130 standard courses, with an attendance of 1700 trainees, but also offers custom-designed courses (180 each year). In 1990, 2750 engineers and technicians were trained by CETIM, coming mainly from SMEs.

CETIM is also strongly involved in cooperation projects with the National Education system. It has agreements with 42 teaching establishments, 23 at secondary level and 19 at college level, and there are 20 ongoing thesis projects in collaboration with 10 universities and engineering schools. CETIM has transferred more than 1250 software packages to educational institutions, which will be used by approximately 140,000 students.

Another important project is the "Coeur de Metier" (heart of the trade) project, which proposes a new educational tool for speeding up the training of machining workers. This ambitious project is being developed jointly by the Association of Mechanical Industries (FIM), the Union of Mining and Metallurgical Industries (UIMM), and the National Education system in order to respond to the industrial requirement for skilled workers.

Information. To publicize the results of its research and development, to keep the industrial sector updated on technological developments, and to offer the means of selection of appropriate techniques, equipments, and materials, CETIM produces a large number of publications, periodicals, videos, etc.

- *200 published titles,* of which 17,000 copies are printed and distributed each year.
- *CETIM—Information,* a magazine created 25 years ago, is published 6 times a year with 15,000 copies per issue. It publicizes the results of the research and development projects carried out and informs about technologies of interest for mechanical engineers and about the activities, products, and services provided by CETIM. It addresses mainly the technical staff of the enterprises.
- *Lettre du CETIM,* created 3 years ago, is published 10 times a year with 10,000 copies per issue. It addresses exclusively the heads of enterprises, who do not always have the time to read lengthier publications.
- *Technologies Mecaniques* appears monthly with a run of 550 copies; it is a bibliographic selection of new technologies and their suppliers and users.

CETIM has an extensive library, comprising 25,000 works and 800 periodicals from France and abroad. CETIM's own bibliographical database has 100,000 entries of specialized papers and is accessible through network connection (ESA-IRS) or is distributed through CDs (MECA-CD). Each year 4000 new entries are added to the database. The technical information center also translates about 4000 papers each year. All these services are freely accessible to everyone.

Software. CETIM has developed and sells 41 software products, providing tools for:

- Design departments
- Methods
- Manufacture
- Control
- Management
- Training

PROGETIM, with offices in Roissy (France), Birmingham (U.K.), and Mannheim (Germany), is responsible for marketing CETIM software packages.

Standardization and certification. CETIM contributes actively to standardization efforts in the mechanical engineering field, participating at the national standardization groups and representing French interests in international working committees.

Owing to CETIM's strong commitment to standardization, 6.1 percent of its yearly budget is applied for supporting this activity. CETIM's concrete actions are:

- Financial support of the Union for Standardization of the Mechanic (UNM)
- Prenormative technical studies
- Technical surveys within work groups
- Constant watch of standardization works (technological watch)
- Development of products facilitating the use of standards (software, publications, training sessions)

CETIM's engineers and technicians participate in over 80 work groups, technical committees, and commissions of the UNM, AFNOR, CEN, and ISO.

CETIM also maintains a strong presence in exhibitions, meetings, and conferences, in France as well as abroad, and has an active promotional activity distributing catalogs, brochures, and technical information sheets and editing an activity report.

Examples of cooperation in CETIM—mechanical enterprises

A flexible machining cell in an SME. The enterprise Colmart Cuvelier Dodge is located in the suburbs of Lille, employs 77 persons, and has a 60-million-franc turnover. It produces different transmission products, mainly pulleys and hubs. In order to achieve production improvement, the company requested CETIM to study the possibility of automating the pulley production, since these products represent a major share of their turnover. CETIM analyzed the company's production from a multidimensional viewpoint, taking into account the manufacturing sequence and charges. This analysis allowed the identification of a hundred or so different products. The next logical step was to find the type of flexible machining cell best suited for solving the problem. The final solution consisted of two CNC lathes, a special two-head multispindle drilling-tapping machine, and a three-axis gantry robot that ensured smooth flow between the workplaces.

The total investment for the equipment was 4 million francs, and it completely satisfied the managers of Colmart Cuvelier Dodge: The lead times have been reduced from 3 weeks to less than a day and the machine utilization has also increased 30 percent as compared to the manually operated NC machines.

Drilling of Inconel and titanium—choice of the right coating. Inconel and titanium are two noble metals, with high mechanical performance and with wide application in the aeronautical sector. Nevertheless the use of these superalloys gives rise to specific difficulties during cutting operations, and in the case of the machining of titanium alloys, there are also contamination problems.

The Balzers company, specializing in metal coatings, was committed to finding a new coating that solved these machining problems: "Our customers and partners are always researching for better production conditions. In order to satisfy their requirements we requested the CETIM, establishment Senlis, which is especially well equipped for this kind of research, to define the best cutting conditions for working with these materials and the optimal life span of the used tools."

The detailed, theoretical study and several tests, yeilded promising conclusions. It was found that for two materials, TA6V and Inconel 718, the best results are obtained using drills with the new coating material Balinit, not only for productivity but also for longer lifetime of the tool.

9

Shared Manufacturing: The American Experience

David M. Porreca

National Institute of Flexible Manufacturing
Meadville, Pa.

Background

The Meadville, Pa., area is located in the center of a 100-mile radius that encompasses Buffalo, Pittsburgh, and Cleveland. It is adjacent to the major north-south highway Route 79, is 40 miles south of Erie, PA, and is located in Crawford County.

The tooling and machining industry, with approximately 150 companies in the area, is Crawford County's largest employer. This industry gives the Meadville area the highest concentration of highly skilled workers and companies per capita in the country. A study done for the local National Tooling and Machining Association in 1988 attributed up to 20 percent of all manufacturing income generated in Crawford County to the industry.

The Meadville area tooling and precision machining industry traces its roots back to Talon, Inc., the premier maker of the zipper. Talon had a tooling operation with 300 employees. To accommodate their training needs, Talon developed an apprentice program in the mid-1900s that was very comprehensive. This apprentice program produced highly skilled graduates with the capability of doing close tolerance work. When much of Talon's market was taken by foreign imports in the sixties and seventies, many of the skilled workers began looking for employment, and many of them became entrepreneurs.

Most of the new manufacturing enterprises these entrepreneurs created, as well as many other manufacturing enterprises in northwest Pennsylvania, are faced with the same dilemma—how to stay competitive when confronted with growing worldwide competition and how to stay current with the latest advanced technologies and management philosophies. Many large corporations that the Meadville companies supply are putting pressure on them to produce more, with better quality and at a better price. The major companies have increasingly shifted design, research, and production decisions to these same suppliers in order to keep their own costs to a minimum. Many suppliers that have chosen not to go along with all the demands of their major customers are no longer suppliers.

Over the years the Polish Alliance College in Cambridge Springs, Pa., and the local vocational-technical school have provided technical training and skilled graduates to the small and medium-sized businesses in the area. However, the financial pressures on academic institutions and the speed and the breadth of change in recent years have surpassed the abilities of these institutions to exist or stay current. Corporations have been spending more and more money to adequately train their own employees because of this problem, but the need has still not been satisfied.

In the spring of 1987, Alliance College announced it would be suspending operations. This development, more than anything perhaps, provided the impetus for a group of businesspeople in the Meadville Area Chamber of Commerce to take action and attempt to address some of the long-standing technical and training needs of the industry. They decided to create a new organization and call it the National Institute of Flexible Manufacturing (NIFM). NIFM was formed as a nonprofit educational and training corporation with the mission to support the acquisition of world-class flexible manufacturing technologies and management techniques by small and medium-sized firms in northwest Pennsylvania. Among the group of businesspeople were an ex-governor of Pennsylvania, Raymond Shafer; Tom Lang, president of Dad's Products in Meadville; and Harold Corner, president of C & J Industries and former president of the National Tooling and Machining Association. Governor Shafer and Tom Lang were not from the industry but were very concerned about the future of Meadville. Corner was from the industry, was aware of what domestic and international firms were doing, and felt that the Meadville firms were in a precarious position. He was also aware of the concept of a shared flexible computer integrated manufacturing facility (FCIM) that had been developed by the Office of Productivity, Technology and Innovation (OPTI), the U.S. Department of Commerce. This model was to be used in developing NIFM. OPTI officials came to Meadville and discussed the FCIM concept with the Meadville businesspeople in the summer of 1987. It was concluded that since this effort would be "private sector driven," the National Institute of Flexible Manufacturing (NIFM) could serve as a national model which could be replicated in other parts of the country.

The Needs Survey

The founders of NIFM envisioned that it should be a teaching factory that would provide the following:

- Education in modern management philosophies such as total quality management and also computer-aided design (CAD), computer-aided manufacturing (CAM), computer integrated manufacturing (CIM), and statistical process control (SPC)
- Hands-on training on modern high-technology machinery and computer hardware
- A demonstration site for new hardware and software
- A shared manufacturing facility with state-of-the-art equipment for use by small and medium-sized firms

Reducing these goals into specific objectives and programs required a more in-depth market analysis. The funding for a feasibility study was provided by the Economic Development Administration of the U.S. Department of Commerce. The objectives of the study were to determine the following:

1. What types of manufacturing companies (size and industry) can best use a shared flexible computer integrated manufacturing (FCIM) facility?
2. What type of product lines lend themselves to a mixed use FCIM facility?
3. What services should the facility provide?
4. What should go into a facility: Manufacturing cells? CAD? MRP capability? Automated handling? Robotics?
5. What should be the minimum volume required to make a system cost-effective and economically viable?
6. What would be the major hurdles that would prevent companies from using a shared facility, and how could these issues be overcome?
7. Who would use the facility? The sharers or an independent outside membership?
8. What would such a facility cost, and how would it be financed? (The building, equipment, personnel, and all other operating expenses needed to be considered.)

Survey forms were developed and sent to 847 manufacturing firms in 14 counties in northwest Pennsylvania. Companies that did not respond to the initial mailing were called, and whenever possible, the information was taken over the phone. The expected rate of return for a blind survey is approximately 10 percent. Of the 847 questionnaires mailed, 244 (28.8 percent) were returned. The majority of the companies that responded were small; over half were producers of metal products with less than $500,000 in sales and fewer than 25 employees.

Since NIFM was to be oriented toward modern technologies, it was important not only to measure the interest of local firms but also to ascertain their current level of involvement with advanced technologies. Part of the information asked for in the survey concerned the type and quantity of their machinery. Of the 128 metal-producing firms that responded, 39.1 percent reported having no NC (numerical control) or CNC (computer numerical controlled) equipment. Over 85 percent of the firms had fewer than 11 NC or CNC machines. (See Table 9.1.)

Another indication of the lack of technological sophistication of the manufacturers surveyed was the way computers were used internally and the fact that not many were used in applications other than accounting. The majority of companies reported having a computer in house (65.3 percent), but they did not appear to be using them effectively in the operational part of their business. Although 46 percent of surveyed companies were using computers for accounting purposes, less than 25 percent of these firms were using computers for any other application (see Table 9.2).

It was clear from the survey that many companies had not successfully adopted new technology or had not successfully implemented it in their business. These factors would have to be taken into consideration as the NIFM planned its educational programs and its machine acquisition.

Getting Started

The two main foci of NIFM were to be educational programs and hands-on training. Because of funding limitations, the educational programs were started first. Programs in total quality management (TQM), statistical process control (SPC), and computer integrated

TABLE 9.1   Types and Number of Metalworking Machines

Total metal-working machines	Manual machines, %	NC-CNC machines, %
0	3.1	39
1–10	19.5	46.1
11–20	25.0	5.5
21–30	16.4	1.6
Over 30	36.0	7.8

TABLE 9.2   Functions Performed by Computer

Function	% Total
Accounting	46.0
CAD	9.2
Inventory control	22.6
Job costing	15.1
Order processing	14.6
Word processing	24.7
Production control	20.9
NC programming	20.1
Materials control	12.6
Database management	13.0

manufacturing (CIM) were typical of some of the initial offerings of the institute.

NIFM used instructors from local universities and other professionals to conduct these courses. It was decided that because of the variety of the courses, it would not be judicious to maintain its own instructors. The hope was that these courses would help to develop some name recognition for NIFM, cover some expenses, and also fund some future activities.

In reality, it was fairly expensive to market and advertise these courses and the profits were fairly low. The courses did, however, give NIFM some exposure, and from that standpoint they were successful. NIFM was not aligned with a university, nor did it have a cooperative agreement with a university. Many shared centers that have recently been established are aligned and, in fact, colocated with universities. These partnerships can be a distinct advantage and should be capitalized on by these new centers.

The university that a center becomes aligned with may or may not already have in place many of the courses the center wishes to present to local businesses. If the courses have already been developed, the arrangements to present them to local businesses should be relatively simple and the cost relatively low. These are obvious advantages to the center. If a course is not available, as might be the case with a course such as Total Quality Management, the center can provide the impetus to get this important course developed. In this case, the center might be instrumental in getting the university to develop a course that is very relevant to local businesses, and therefore should be very important to the university. As an example of this, many businesses across the country have been practicing TQM for more than 5 years, yet it is not uncommon to find a university that does not teach it.

Machinery Acquisition

Once the educational programs were initiated, efforts turned to acquiring the necessary equipment to give small and medium-sized companies an opportunity to get hands-on training. Funding from the Office of Technology Development, Department of Commerce of the state of Pennsylvania, enabled NIFM to consider leasing several pieces of equipment, and a machine selection committee of potential NIFM users was formed.

The first piece of equipment the committee decided on was a Charmilles Roboform 400. The decision to get this piece of equipment was driven by the fact that the technology was very important to the area and that one local company guaranteed it would use the piece for a significant number of hours over the first year.

Not everyone on the committee agreed that the chosen piece was the right one, but it turned out that the revenues generated by the rental of this piece over the first 3 years were very critical to NIFM's survival. Had this company not paid the fees it did on this piece of equipment over a 3-year period, NIFM most likely would not have succeeded. So whereas the selection of the first piece of equipment was somewhat controversial, in the long run it turned out to be a very crucial one for NIFM.

The negotiations leading to the agreement to get the first piece of equipment were not without problems. NIFM did not have any credibility, nor did it have a credit history. The concept of shared manufacturing was brand new and no one knew if it would work. There was no one on the NIFM staff who knew how to operate or maintain a piece of sophisticated machinery. Fortunately, Charmilles Technology, the first manufacturer selected, turned out to be an excellent one. They understood the situation and felt so strongly about what we were doing that they decided to take a chance on NIFM.

Problems

In the initial planning stages of NIFM, it was thought that the manufacturers of machine tools would be anxious to display and demonstrate their equipment at NIFM. This was a bit naive in that many costs are associated with owning, transporting, and demonstrating equipment, and the manufacturers had no reason to believe that displaying the equipment at NIFM would provide any benefits.

Another problem encountered in the early stages was the concern among local shops that the institute would compete with them by making parts and by spawning a number of new competitors for them. It was particularly annoying to some small shop owners to think that part of their tax money would be used to support an organization that would compete with them or would supply equipment to someone who would compete with them (and do it with more advanced equipment). It was not really made clear in the early stages who would be producing what at NIFM, and with all the high-technology equipment, it was understandable that some would view it as a threat.

As NIFM began its marketing efforts with door-to-door selling of its services, it was clear that the issue of NIFM being a competitor was not going to go away. It also became clear that unless the issue of competition could be resolved, NIFM was going to have a hard time attracting a sufficient number of users. This issue caused NIFM to think through its position on "competing" and also to reaffirm some policies that in fact had already been in effect.

Up to that point, all the production work being done at NIFM was being done by customers. The NIFM staff was not making any components for resale and in fact did not have the support staff to be quoting, inspecting, etc. The role of the NIFM staff was a training role and staff members were restricted to this activity. The position to the customers became "we don't produce anything, we train." This was the message conveyed to the users and prospective users, and NIFM did not have to change the way it operated because it never was competing. The perception, not the reality, was the problem. Over a period of time, this explanation seemed to deflect the criticism on competition. Another problem at the outset was an identity problem. Few people understood what NIFM was or what it was supposed to do. The educational programs were intended to acquaint people with NIFM, but that did not help with those shops that never attended the programs. In an attempt to correct this problem, a brochure and a newsletter were produced, and an extensive effort was made to work through industry-related organizations such as the NTMA, SME, and APICS. These efforts were successful in helping to acquaint people with NIFM.

Notable Successes

After having started out with a single piece of production equipment and two computers and having only two pieces of production equipment for the first 2 years, NIFM was able to quickly increase to six pieces of production equipment by the middle of the third year. It has now established that unquantifiable "credibility" with a number of manufacturers and is in the process of adding more equipment. Agreements have been reached with a number of manufacturers that will allow NIFM to upgrade the equipment as the technology changes.

One of the key elements of establishing a good working relationship with various manufacturers is the attitude of partnership.

NIFM recognizes that the manufacturers may want to conduct demonstrations and seminars on the equipment, so manufacturers may use the facility at no charge. In fact, NIFM staff often helps with the demonstrations. Specific pieces of equipment are not recommended to the users; however, positive or negative experiences are related to the users. Manufacturers are told it is their job to sell equipment and the NIFM's job to transfer technology. These two objectives can be mutually inclusive.

To date, NIFM users have operated and leased its equipment for over 10,000 hours. During that time they have learned how to operate the equipment, have taken on and completed jobs more economically and more efficiently than ever before, have done some jobs they previously could not do, have learned from other shops which they previously regarded simply as competitors, and have justified and purchased new high-technology equipment. These results were all anticipated in a shared center, and they have been realized.

The educational program has also been successful. Employees of more than 50 shops have participated in at least one of our programs. The center has developed a customized SPC course for small shops, has worked with Penn State to get a series of Quality courses conducted at NIFM, and has worked with the local APICS chapter and a number of consultants to offer a full range of courses on Master Scheduling and Total Quality Management.

Another avenue pursued, similar to the cooperative arrangements with the manufacturers, is cooperative arrangements with several universities. NIFM was a coapplicant with Gannon University to IBM and was accepted into the IBM CIM for Higher Education Program. This relationship with both Gannon and IBM allows NIFM access to a sophisticated computer system, over a million dollars worth of software, and the expertise of the Gannon University faculty. NIFM is also working closely with Edinboro University and is in the process of developing a Certificate Program in Tooling and Precision Machining.

Lessons Learned

Marketing is undoubtedly not the first thing that comes to mind when a group or an individual considers setting up a shared center. The availability of a facility, qualified personnel, equipment, and funding are likely to be discussed in great detail. At some point the needs of the "customer" or "user" of the facility will be considered, but usually this comes later in the planning process.

A survey or needs assessment was done for NIFM as part of the feasibility study. In retrospect, many of the findings in the survey did not appear to have had a significant influence on the programs or on the design of NIFM. The educational programs and the equipment that people had in mind before the needs assessment were close to what was eventually decided on after the assessment. These decisions are fine if the assessment simply corroborates the information already in hand, but this is not likely.

When it was discovered that 39 percent of the firms that replied did not have CNC equipment, the planned program should probably have been started on a much more basic level. The centers need to be "customer-driven," much like any business. If they are not "customer-driven," the need for their services is not likely to justify their existence. The initial needs assessment may be considered to be the first step in the marketing of the center. As with any other business, marketing must be established as a functional branch of the center. The technology and educational needs are changing so quickly that each center must be constantly monitoring the needs of industry in its respective area.

Another factor that makes marketing so crucial is the centers continual need to replace its biggest users after they have purchased their own equipment and at least temporarily cut back on the hours they are using the equipment at the center. The center hopes to continue to provide technology and educational programs that will be attractive to a variety of companies so that even after they have upgraded part of their operation, they will find use for other programs.

The importance of marketing and the need to emphasize marketing, not only in the initial planning stages of the center but also throughout the operational stage, were probably the most important lessons learned after the first several years of operation. Another important lesson learned in developing NIFM was to have a "realistic" plan. Everything from the cost of the building to the cost of insurance must be considered in the pro forma. Also, assumptions should not be made that companies will immediately sign up for educational programs or immediately put equipment to work two shifts a day, seven days a week. During the marketing survey, probing questions should be asked, as opposed to accepting mere expressions of interest. For example, in the initial needs assessment, a question might be, "If we had a specific piece of equipment, how many hours a month would you be willing to lease it at $30 an hour?" as opposed to asking, "What type of equipment would you like to see at the center?"

It also must be kept in mind that training hours are different from production hours and that the shared use of a piece of equipment by several companies can be a very inefficient process. This will undoubtedly cut into machine revenues, despite the best plan conceived. By being realistic with the planning, centers can avoid overspending on capital equipment, avoid getting trapped with more overheads than can be supported, and avoid creating unrealistic expectations.

Generic Advice

A shared manufacturing facility can provide access to educational programs and high-technology equipment for small and medium-sized companies, which are an important part of the manufacturing community. However, the center must be carefully planned, configured, and managed so as to ensure that it fits the needs of its particular market. The following suggestions are offered:

- Do an in-depth needs assessment of your marketplace. Test your survey instrument on 15 to 20 companies, and make sure you are getting useful data before you send it out to the rest of the businesses.

- Be sure that you have a committed number of users before you decide on any piece of equipment. Be certain that companies are willing to provide students before offering any educational programs.

- Don't overestimate the amount of machine revenues you will be able to generate from users. Scheduling is difficult and training time is not like straight production. You may be treated like a subcontractor and not used when the companies' own machines are not busy.

- Establish good working relationships with as many providers of CNC equipment, computer hardware, and computer software as possible. This technology changes quickly, and you want to keep updating your equipment, hardware, and software as often as possible. A good relationship often means more willingness on the manufacturers' part to help you upgrade as economically as possible.

- Keep your overheads low. Like any other business just starting out, it will take you time to build a customer base and in the meantime, you will have a lot of start-up expenses.

- Seek out those agencies that are trying to help small businesses, and see if they will give you their support. Shared centers can be an excellent resource for small businesses.

- Work with groups of companies and associations whenever possible. They can get the word out to their members and assist you in your marketing effort.

- Establish a good working relationship with local 4-year and 2-year colleges. They can help you with your educational programs and are always looking for ways to interface with small businesses.

You can bring them together with small business and all three parties can benefit.

- Understand your local, state, and federal politics. You are working on a project which can have a great effect on an important part of their constituency, and the political leaders might be willing to help you. If you don't let them know what you're doing, they could hurt you.

Conclusion

The concept of shared flexible computer integrated manufacturing (shared FCIM) was developed in the early 1980s, but its practical application has only been tried in the past several years. The real-life application of shared FCIM, as experienced at the Meadville center, has turned out to be somewhat different from originally conceived but nevertheless has proved to be very beneficial to small and medium-sized firms.

It was theorized that the adoption of "FCIM cells" by small and medium-sized companies could help them compete in today's global market. At the Meadville center a number of companies have adopted FCIM technology but have not adopted FCIM cells. They upgraded their technology and became more efficient, but they have not gotten to the point where they are operating cells. In those shared centers where cells have been installed, the utilization has been low. It is unclear at this point whether or not FCIM cells will be successfully adopted by many small and medium-sized companies, but it is apparent that the adoption of FCIM technology has been very beneficial to the companies.

According to the theory, another benefit of the "shared center" would be the access it provides small and medium companies to high-technology equipment. Many companies never had the opportunity to use high-technology equipment before, but they are using it at Meadville. They are using the equipment to produce actual parts, and many of the personnel at these companies are getting an excellent understanding of what this technology can do for their company. In a number of cases, the companies have purchased new technology after their experience with it at the center.

The opportunity for a number of small companies to share the use and the high initial investment required for modern technology was another reason for developing shared centers. The experience at Meadville has been that companies can successfully share equipment. Their largest concern is scheduling, and the center has been able to accommodate them in the majority of instances. The enthusiasm of shops regarding the sharing of equipment does not seem to extend to sharing in the purchase of the equipment. When it has been proposed that a group of these companies invest in a single piece of equipment and share it, the response has not been very encouraging.

In the original concept of shared centers, training and education were to be extremely important. Training and education have turned out to be the key areas of activity at the Meadville shared center and, in fact, drive the other activities. Factory schools have often provided the impetus for companies to start using new equipment, and other educational programs have been just as instrumental in convincing small companies of the need for change. College students participating in the center as interns have had an opportunity to get "hands-on" training that complements their classroom education and have commented on the importance of it to their overall educational experience.

The production of actual parts has been another important part of the success of NIFM. When the concept of shared manufacturing was first considered, a number of suggestions were made on how to finance the operation. As it turned out, the production of actual parts is not only important to help pay the center's bills, but it also provides the users an opportunity to produce parts for their customers and determine if the quality is satisfactory and the costs reasonable. Normally, a company would only be able to determine their customer's acceptance of the parts produced on a new piece of equipment after a company had already committed to buy the piece. A number of companies have ended up buying the wrong piece of equipment under these circumstances. In the shared center, there is an excellent chance that the companies will have already developed their customer base and will have lined up a good amount of work for the equipment when it gets there.

At the federal, state, and local levels, a significant amount of money is being spent and efforts are being made on behalf of "economic development." Many of these efforts are aimed at improving the competitiveness of manufacturing firms. Shared FCIM centers, because of their hands-on methodology and their emphasis on state-of-the-art technology and management philosophies, are a very cost-effective way to spend economic development dollars. The initial investment in a shared center and the cost to maintain a shared center can be significant. However, much of the cost can be shared with users, educational institutions, manufacturers, and federal, state, and local agencies.

On those occasions when companies have worked together at NIFM, the learning that transpires is exciting. Attempts are being made to broaden the appeal of NIFM, including a new needs assessment which is currently being conducted.

Bibliography

Demirai, Sezai, and Michael Hannon, "Initial Study on the Economic Impact of Tooling and Machining in Northwestern Pennsylvania," October 1988.

Department of Commerce Letter, August 1987.

"Market Assessment for a Metalworking Flexible Manufacturing System," Technology Management Group, September 1988, p. 18.

National Institute of Flexible Manufacturing (NIFM) report to the U.S. Department of Commerce—Economic Development Administration, Apr. 12, 1989.

10

Strategic
Alternatives for
Competitiveness

There is no question that small and midsized manufacturers play a significant role in the global economy. These manufacturers face many competitive threats; the use of outdated manufacturing equipment is one of their more important dilemmas. A nation's standard of living depends to a large degree on the competitiveness of these manufacturers. If their capabilities are not improved through the availability of modern manufacturing systems technology, their economic well-being may well decline.

For example, outmoded manufacturing techniques account for approximately 85 percent of the difficulties facing U.S. manufacturers.[1]

These small firms are focused on economies of scale through single-function mass-production strategies—an inadequate strategy today considering the complicated tasks required in manufacturing the complex products currently in demand. The production technology of the past cannot provide the manufacturing need for programmable automation alone.

Small and midsized manufacturers all too often lack the financing, expertise, and time needed to learn more about modern manufacturing systems technology. Consultants' fees are often too high for these firms to bear. In the past the U.S. government has provided notoriously modest funding support to aid these small firms. If the small and midsized manufacturers do launch manufacturing technology improvements that involve substantial funding, the cost of choosing the wrong technology is very risky—a risk that these firms simply are not willing (and cannot afford) to take. They tend to continue to "muddle through" with a technology that is not globally competitive. In addition, the cutbacks in spending in the defense industry reduce the options available to small and midsized manufacturers who have served as suppliers to defense OEMs.

Assistance Needed

States have provided some assistance to manufacturers through programs akin to the U.S. Department of Agriculture Extension Programs. These programs have provided a wide range of activities such as consultancy, referrals, on-site evaluations, workshops, seminars, and distribution of newsletters and other mailings. The federal government's support of the development of technology to improve quality and to modernize manufacturing processes took a significant step in the Omnibus Trade and Competitiveness Act of 1988 which renamed the National Bureau of Standards the National Institute of Standards and Technology (NIST). The establishment of manufacturing technology centers through cooperative agreements with nonprofit extension services at the state and local level was a much needed step in improving U.S. competitiveness. Other initiatives have been launched by the federal government, which on balance has not been effective in sufficiently enhancing the competitiveness of small and midsized manufacturers.

Strategic Investments

The 360,000 small and midsized manufacturers in the United States must be supported by strategic investments of low-cost capital in modern plant, equipment, and human resources. Even the availability of low-cost capital is beyond the resources of all too many manufacturers. What strategies are available to the entrepreneur who has marketable products but is saddled with outmoded plant and equipment, untrained people, and who has insufficient capital to make even minimal investments? Help from state or federal sources at best is probabilistic—what is needed is a local center where collaboration between small and midsized users, government, and academia can provide a means for resource sharing. Resource sharing through the manufacturing assistance centers can provide the opportunity to build strategic partnerships at the national, state, and local levels to provide assistance to these small entrepreneurs.

The question facing government and industry today is this: Should the United States have a strategic industrial policy to nurture and promote technology and industry? Most forward-thinking industrialists would agree that the United States needs a vision directed toward the global economy of the 1990s. The boosting of research spending across a wide range of technologies, a change in the tax laws that makes it advantageous to invest in research, development, and equipment, and providing the opportunity for small businesses to get assistance to learn the latest manufacturing techniques are some of the options available in any industrial policy. Governments at all levels—federal, state, and local—must speed the transfer of contemporaneous manufacturing systems technology to our nation's small and midsized manufacturers.

The Challenges

Consider the challenges that face U.S. manufacturers: Over the past 30 years U.S. manufacturing has fallen from 28 percent of gross national product to 19 percent. During this same period manufacturing employment dropped from 23 percent of the total employment base to 14 percent. Today, for the first time in U.S. history, more people are working in local, state, and federal government than in manufacturing—and experts predict that by 1996, Japan will outproduce the United States in manufacturing.[2]

The manufacturing sector in the United States shed 675,000 jobs during the 1980s; another 1.1 million jobs were lost during the recession that occurred at the end of the 1980s. Industrial corporations, which generally provide the best wages and benefits, have been cutting work forces. The *Fortune* 500 industrial companies employed 3.7 million fewer workers in 1991 than the top 500 firms did in 1981—a loss of about one job in four. Hardly any forecaster expects manufacturing to get back to its already diminished prerecession employment levels.

Most smaller companies see little advantage in assuming the cost of worker training themselves. Many workers spent their careers doing routine assembly work and had little skill in teamwork, communication, numerical analysis, or the ability to run sophisticated machine tools and the creative and innovative know-how to organize work. Some companies have teamed up with local colleges to help prepare young students for high-skill jobs to include visits to factories to acquire a feel for the course work and training they will need. Some companies plan to give on-the-job training as early as the eleventh year. The challenge: bringing together an increasingly sophisticated manufacturing system designed by intelligent creative people coming out of high school whose skills are all too often minimal or lacking altogether. This in the face of a growing global marketplace where a higher premium is put on efficient and flexible manufacturing systems.

In Germany most firms participate in an apprenticeship program to prepare employees for work. Some of these programs last 4 years or more; 60 percent of German youth ages 16 to 18 become apprentices. Companies, industry councils, and labor unions participate in the design of these programs. Not only do workers learn new skills in these apprenticeship programs; information on how to organize work better is shared among companies—and the incentive to raid individual employees who invest more in training is reduced.[3]

Strategic Issues

Key strategic issues facing the manufacturing industry in the United States include the ability to commercialize technology sooner, manufacture and service quality products, design products and services for global markets, and incorporate emerging state-of-the-art manufacturing systems technology into products and services. A deficit-induced ceiling on government spending and a Washington-based industrial policy that heretofore eschews government assistance beyond token dollars reduce the global competitiveness of small and midsized manufacturers in the United States.

The U.S. manufacturing infrastructure is in a critical stage of decline. During the past several years global competitiveness has impacted the product and process strategy of manufacturing establishments all over the world. All too many U.S. manufacturers' assets are suffering from years of neglect, overuse, and deferred maintenance, repair, and replacement because of inadequate capital for strategic investments by small and midsized manufacturers. U.S. manufacturers are losing their competitive advantage to international competitors. Major competitors in Japan, Germany, and other industrialized countries are showing productivity improvement and the utilization of state-of-the-art manufacturing systems technology to leverage productivity and quality improvements. According to one report, "America now ranks 55th in the world in capital investment in infrastructure."[4] Infrastructure spending has become increasingly localized with reduced support from federal and state governments. Both political parties during the 1992 federal elections promised to provide support to make American industry more competitive. The Clinton administration's manufacturing initiatives show promise. We are encouraged.

Free Trade

The world is moving to global business because of increasing economic interdependence and reduced barriers to the flow of information, finances, and technology. A United Europe, new nations and economies in the Soviet bloc region, emerging trade regions in the Western Hemisphere and the Pacific Rim, and the political and economic mellowing of China have created enormous economic opportunities. Risks, uncertainties, technological innovation, and financial needs are going beyond even the reach of any single multinational. New alliances are being formed in almost every area of multinational business—from investment to production to finance and to marketing.

The competitive dimensions in manufacturing will likely change as a result of the free trade agreements forming among nations in the world. In the Western Hemisphere completion of the North American Free Trade Agreement (NAFTA) will change the manner of doing business with Canada and Mexico. Mexico's 5-year campaign for economic reform will accelerate—to include opening the way for an increase of new investments in its rapidly modernizing economy. U.S. factories will have accelerated access to Mexico. At the present time Mexico is the fastest-growing market for American goods and services. In 1991, Mexico acquired $33 billion of U.S. exports, becoming America's third-biggest customer—likely soon to surpass No. 2 Japan. Access to Mexico will provide opportunities for U.S. manufacturers to divert some jobs to that country.[5]

President Carlos Salinas of Mexico has provided the leadership for a program administered by Nacional Financiera, the government development bank, to provide support to small and medium-sized business firms. In 1991, financial support was provided for more than 100,000 new small and medium-sized firms to include technological packages and commercial education. The economic program fostered by President Salinas has surprised the world with its speed and momentum.[6]

Industrial Policy

Sadly the United States no longer leads the world in the exploitation of technology—turning the technology into competitive products and services. The U.S. track record in innovation and funding basic research has come to depend on picking up ideas generated in the United States and commercializing them into marketable products and services. This commercialization is dependent on a complex integration of economics, trade, regulatory policies, competitive verve, as well as management and manufacturing capability.

Some forward thinkers in the United States have suggested that a National Industrial Extension Service for technology and manufacturing be created, similar to the successful extension service championed so effectively by the U.S. Department of Agriculture. Small and midsized manufacturing enterprises could benefit greatly from a manufacturing extension service to help in the transfer of manufacturing systems technology within local communities.

George Fisher, CEO of Motorola, told a Chicago audience: "Our principal rivals today are no longer military. They are those who pursue economic, technological, and industrial policies designed to expand their shares of global markets. This is the way it is. U.S. policy must reflect this reality if we are to remain a world leader and role model." The Center for Security Policy, in a report released in March, urged the federal government "...to take a proactive role in identifying technological needs and opportunities...and to work cooperatively with industry and universities to develop new, advanced and enabling technologies in those areas deemed to be critical to U.S. economic competitiveness." Manufacturing systems technology is an "enabling technology" deemed to be critical to U.S. economic competitiveness. Mastery of such technology is clearly critical to the survival of small and midsized manufacturers in the United States. Far too many lag behind in such technology. Some experts estimate that outdated manufacturing practices are pervasive and account for about 85 percent of the problems of American firms.

Changing Work Force

Human resource development in manufacturing will play a key role in separating those companies who are winners and those who are losers. Advanced manufacturing practices today require employees with a unique blend of competencies and knowledge—over the next decade these competencies and knowledge will become even more sophisticated. Jobs that will be created over the next decade will require people who have education beyond high school and over 30 percent will require a college education.

Manufacturers need "systems assistance" in the sense of updated plant and equipment, enlightened management, and improved human resources. Insight into the human side of manufacturing can be gained by perusal of a study supported by the Washington-based Council on Competitiveness. The council is a private organization made up of representatives of high-tech companies, with a smattering of academic and labor notables. The study performed at the Harvard Business School under management professor Michael Porter concluded that with some exceptions, U.S. industry has been allocating its capital incorrectly. The study says that U.S. companies are being outperformed by their German and Japanese counterparts who stress factors U.S. corporate managers see as "soft"—such factors as employee training, human resource development, relations with suppliers, information systems, and organizational development. These investments for the "softer" assets of doing business are important—but are hard to assess for their impact on the bottom line.[7]

Conclusion

Clearly world-class manufacturing is being driven by continuous change in the development and application of manufacturing systems technology. The manufacturing of today will not be the manufacturing of the future—the global competitive playing field is changing at a frightening rate. The strategic challenges facing all U.S. manufacturers are clear. For small and midsized manufacturers these challenges, if not met, will result in the continued inability of these manufacturers to survive.

The challenges facing U.S. manufacturers are awesome. Not only is manufacturing systems technology changing as global competitors become more adept at creating and applying new technology; the work force and its needs and competencies are changing as well. The development of free trade strategies in the world today will pose challenges for U.S. manufacturers they have not had to face before. The development of strategic alliances by manufacturing firms all over the world is introducing new dimensions of competitiveness.

In the face of these changes there is continuing clamor for accelerated government assistance. The U.S. government and some state governments have instituted strategic initiatives to provide help to small and midsized manufacturers. However, we believe that this help may well not go beyond the modest stage—and that the most effective help will be that developed around a *network of manufacturing assistance centers* facilitated by federal, state, and local government support. Self-help thus becomes the most viable strategy for the American manufacturing community—and as that self-help is focused through shared manufacturing centers the global competitiveness of small and midsized manufacturers will surely improve.

If the competitiveness of these manufacturers is not improved, there is the likelihood that: (1) The United States standard of living will decline; (2) the United States may very well decline in overall economic power; (3) the United States will continue to be more of a *service* economy; and (4) overall U.S. global competitiveness will decline.

We believe that much can be done to improve the competitiveness of small and midsized manufacturers through the development of a network of manufacturing assistance centers in the United States. Such centers can provide manufacturing systems technology assistance by providing a local facility for state-of-the-art equipment and manufacturing systems and processes, as well as improved human competencies that make the modern factory an ongoing productive system. Manufacturers—and other agencies such as educational institutions—will be provided a place to regain and maintain their competitiveness.

Finally, we note with guarded optimism, some of the strategic initiatives in manufacturing systems technology coming forth from the new Administration in Washington, D.C. If these initiatives are successful, U.S. manufacturing could improve—and in the process become more competitive.

References

1. Farrell, Christopher, et al., "Industrial Policy," *Business Week,* Apr. 6, 1992, pp. 70–76.
2. *Focus,* National Center for Manufacturing Sciences, May 1992.
3. Paraphrased from O'Reilly, Brian, "The Job Drought," *Fortune,* Aug. 24, 1992, pp. 62–74.
4. "Facing the Crisis," *Constructor,* June 1989, p. 27.
5. Bacon, Kenneth H., "With Free-Trade Pact About Wrapped Up, The Real Battle Begins," *Wall Street Journal,* Aug. 7, 1992.
6. *Forbes,* Aug. 17, 1992.
7. *C&EN,* June 29, 1992, pp. 21–22.

Index

ABOUT THE AUTHORS

BOPAYA BIDANDA is an associate professor of industrial engineering at the University of Pittsburgh. He is a coeditor, with Professor Cleland, of *The Automated Factory Handbook: Technology and Management*. Professor Bidanda is a senior member of the Institute of Industrial Engineers and the Society of Manufacturing Engineers.

DAVID I. CLELAND is an Ernest E. Roth professor and professor of engineering management at the University of Pittsburgh. He is author and editor of 22 books on management topics, including *Project Management: Strategic Design and Implementation*, published by McGraw-Hill.

SHRIRAM R. DHARWADKAR is an associate professor at South Carolina University, where he has taught courses in project managment, operations research, and quality control. He is completing a dissertation on the assessment of user needs in the design and configuration of shared manufacturing centers.